Kim McCabe is the founder of Rites for Girls. As the originator and facilitator of Girls Journeying Together groups, she offers guidance to preteen and teen girls and simultaneous support for their mothers. In training other women to facilitate these groups, her dream is that every girl grows up expecting to be supported and celebrated in adolescence. Kim was commissioned to write a section in Steve Biddulph's latest best-selling book, *10 Things Girls Need Most: To Grow Up Strong and Free*.

Kim is a home-educating mother of two boys, one girl, two cats and a colony of aloe vera plants; she is wife to a Kiwi, daughter to itinerant parents, friend to a cherished few, and lover of time alone, too. She lives in the Ashdown Forest in Sussex. She sometimes shouts at her children, accidentally steps on the cat's tail and forgets to water the plants, but she loves her work, her family and her life. She has always had deep affinity with teenage girls, and by sharing her wisdom and compassion she infects the reader with her enthusiasm for this life stage.

Other titles

From Daughter to Woman

Parenting girls safely through their teens

Kim McCabe

....

A HOW TO BOOK

To my mother and my daughter

ROBINSON

First published in Great Britain in 2018 by
Robinson

10 9 8 7 6 5 4 3 2 1

A CIP catalogue record for this book
is available from the British Library.

ISBN: 978-1-40871-021-0

Typeset in Sentinel by
Initial Typesetting Services, Edinburgh
Printed and bound in Great Britain by CPI
Group (UK), Croydon CR0 4YY

Papers used by Robinson are from well-
managed forests and other responsible
sources.

Robinson
An imprint of
Little, Brown Book Group
Carmelite House
50 Victoria Embankment
London EC4Y 0DZ

An Hachette UK Company
www.hachette.co.uk

www.littlebrown.co.uk

....

How To Books are published by Robinson,
an imprint of Little, Brown Book Group. We
welcome proposals from authors who have
first-hand experience of their subjects.
Please set out the aims of your book, its target
market and its suggested contents in an email
to Nikki.Read@howtobooks.co.uk

....

CONTENTS

Part II
The chaos of adolescence

Foreword

Sitting with Kim McCabe in her living room, deep in the Sussex woods, there are two competing impressions: she is still and calm, but somehow on fire. You catch the blaze in her eyes and the intensity of concern that she feels for the young. Especially for girls on the cusp of adolescence, still vulnerable but still spirited, too, and not yet crushed by society's grinding pressure over looks, performance, and being an object for evaluation by boys and men.

Kim is the creator of an extraordinary social advance: the idea of coming-of-age groups for girls which are of serious duration, at least a year long, intense and separate from their usual friendship groups (which can be such a mixed blessing as every parent of daughters knows). Parents, especially mothers, are also involved in these groups, visiting from time to time to share the learnings of womanhood, the wounds and stumbles of adolescence, and affirming and strengthening the uniqueness of each girl. Because young people are not cookie cutter clones of each other, conforming to ever-narrower ideas of what shape, size, clothing, face, interests and ambitions are handed down to them. We need a million different ways to be a woman, and a man, if our species is to survive. And that means supporting the young tender shoots of individuality when they need it the most.

The core message that Kim teaches – one which brought a startling rush of tears to my eyes as it echoed into the pain of my own adolescence, and that of every battered and bruised young person I have ever known – is that **you don't have to fit in**. In Kim's work, being accepted as you is the fiercely defended core belief, and the girls in the groups, as they gradually absorb this, become freer and freer, hopefully for the rest of their lives. It's no wonder there are girls queuing up, and coming from across the country, to have this in their lives. And that concerned women are queuing up to learn how to bring this to their own communities from across the world.

That then, is the starting point of this book. While not everyone can have what Kim and her group of educators offer, the ideas are shareable and easy to understand, in your home, with your girl, now. There are hundreds of pieces of information and wisdom in the culture about raising girls into women and they are gathered here in abundance. This book will get you started, and who knows where it will lead.

I've been writing and reading parenting books for forty years. So I know what it's like. You stand in front of the crowded shelves, and sigh. You buy a book or three, often before your baby is born, or just after. Some you read, others you never get around to. But as challenges arise, or time allows, you start to dip in. And then something happens . . .

You end up with one book, whose author's voice you grow to like and trust. They become something more than a friend, more of a stern but warm auntie, uncle or grandfather, with twinkling eyes and infinite patience, and enormous street-smarts – along with a willingness to kick your backside that only adds to the sense of security. Here is firm ground. This road has been travelled before. I don't have to do it on my own.

Kim's is this kind of book. Don't take my word for it, just dip in and you will find out for yourself. Here is a friend for the teenage years that will help you in uncountable ways. I can't believe how much depth and the range of ideas Kim has put into one book.

Have you any idea what it's like to be a girl today, if she is not given deep emotional support, strong companionship of family and friends, patient nurturing from parents who have her back?

It's like being out in a bleak open place, with a cold wind blowing, and the darkness closing in all around you. And hyenas circling in the shadows. Girlhood has become lonelier, even with all the tweets, instagrams and likes. Boys have turned ugly, school has become a nightmare of pressure, and life looks at you with critical eyes and finds you wanting.

Ours is a society that treats us all as products, and girls with their sensitive antennae for the social atmosphere, their instinctive wish to connect and collaborate, are suddenly the most vulnerable. That's right: their strengths have become vulnerabilities, because the world wants us anxious, where we will earn, spend, conform and dance to the corporate consumerist tune.

Of course there are the bastions of life – family, community, friendship, shared spirituality, ordinary caring people who look at the young with gentle eyes – but those are all in decline. Family break-ups, relocation, urban life, busyness, fragmentation of our lives from other generations . . . all tear at what holds us up and makes us free and strong.

A movement is growing against this. People are becoming heart-centred and putting human value above things, possessions, luxury and consumption. And they are starting to do what we almost let go of – and outsourced. They are starting to care for the young. In the UK, America and Australia, I meet these strong communities who form a resistance movement to the destruction and despair of our times. They value what is human and special and rare. And at the centre of that, they value our young ones, the hope of us all. There isn't anything that matters more.

I hope this book gets as close to your heart as it did to mine, both as a dad and as someone who cares deeply about all young people everywhere.

We have work to do!

Steve Biddulph, best-selling author and psychologist

Preface

In my early twenties, I counselled distressed teenagers. One girl couldn't stop eating as she tried to numb the grief of losing her mother to cancer. Another arrived each week with yet another piercing or tattoo, until she turned to repeatedly cutting the word 'alone' into the skin on her arm. There was a sixteen-year-old who told me of one sexual encounter after another, none of which she enjoyed, as she tried to make sense of the advances her uncle had made when she was ten. They all hated themselves, were crippled by anxiety and found life impossible to live. Barely out of my teens and nursing my own eating disorder, I wondered how to prevent all this suffering. I vowed to look for a way.

Thirty years later, I am a mother of teenagers and I have a preteen daughter. I founded Rites for Girls, which includes Girls Journeying Together, a programme to support groups of preteen girls to prepare for adolescence and be guided safely through their teens; Rites for Girls International Facilitator Training, which furthers my vision to offer Girls Journeying Together worldwide; and coaching to support mothers in creating rites of passage for their daughters. Born out of my research as an undergraduate student at Cambridge University, my work has evolved through decades of experience with preteens, teenagers, parents and young adults.

I could provide a long list of reasons why life is so much more difficult for teens now than it was. I could scare you with grim statistics of the growing number of teens running into serious problems, developing eating disorders, cutting, suffering anxiety and depression, drinking too much, turning to drugs, getting pregnant, becoming addicted to social media, or failing at school. There's so much to read on how teens are messing up and opting out. I wrote the book because of this deeply worrying stuff. However, it's not a book about what to do if it happens to your teen, but about what to do so that it *won't* happen to her. It will still help you understand more about how to support her if she has run into difficulties.

But let's remember that the majority of teenagers do just fine. Most emerge as decent adults, with a bit of hair-raising life experience, but perhaps better for it. When we focus on the overwhelmingly negative information about teenagers, we tend to lose sight that the teen years can be the most wonderful time of self-exploration and discovery. Teenagers are exciting, thought-provoking, vulnerable and sweet (although they must never hear us calling them 'sweet'). I support parents, particularly mothers of daughters, to embrace the potential of their child's teenage years. These can be a fulfilling time of increasing closeness, even as they move away.

· ·

My aim in this book is to make the adolescent girl's journey just that bit safer, kinder and better supported – so parents and teens can enjoy the teenage years more.

· ·

We fail our children if we only focus on teaching them algebra or what befell the wives of King Henry VIII – and leave discussion of the fundamental issues of maturation up to chance chats with family, the dysfunctional drama of soaps and films, and the immature influence of peers. We give swimming lessons before diving into the sea and driving lessons are mandatory before taking to the roads solo. So let's also insist on structured adult support in preparing our children for adulthood. Most religions and many traditional cultures still recognise the importance of guiding children safely towards adulthood and offer them a rite of passage while they are actively engaged in this maturation process. The more 'developed' we become, the more we abandon our teenagers. We leave them to invent their own idealisations for adulthood and to make their own markers to prove their maturity, often using drink, sex and other risk-taking activities. In this book I make a case for recreating this pivotal rite of passage – helping to prevent all manner of ill-advised teenage behaviour and addressing many teenage mental health issues. I'll provide you with a how-to guide for creating a coming-of-age celebration that is meaningful and acceptable to a modern teen girl.

I dream of a world where girls understand their place in the bigger picture of life; where they can be sure that they will be supported by their community; where they can grow up secure in the knowledge that they will be taught the skills needed for adult life; and, as they become young women, they will also receive the acknowledgement they crave that they are no longer regarded as children by their elders. In turn, they will contribute and support the next generation of girls as they grow into women.

This book is for anyone who wants to help steer our girls happily through their teens. Although it is addressed to and was primarily written as a guidebook for mothers of daughters aged eight to eighteen as they navigate the rocky teenage landscape with their daughters, it is also for anyone concerned with the lives of teenage girls – dads, flummoxed grandmothers and aunties, carers, teachers, youth workers, sports instructors, 'fairy godmothers', as well as those who work with preteen and teenage girls in a personal way. This is also a book for our society, for the community services that are already overstretched and underfunded and shouldn't have to cope with our girls filling holding cells in police stations, hospitals, trauma counsellors' offices . . . and even funeral parlours.

Not all girls have their mothers around as they grow up. Some girls are raised by their dads or live with grandparents or other carers. For a girl to feel loved is far more important than the gender, age or relation of her main caregivers. If you are a 'mother figure' in a girl's life, then this book is also written with you in mind. I hope it is written in a way that will enable you to translate it to fit your situation.

In this book I will show how:

- Mother–Daughter Dates will help you to maintain a healthy relationship with your daughter through adolescence.
- You can guide your daughter robustly towards womanhood by giving her practical information about what lies ahead, helping her to know herself, manage her feelings, hold on to her dreams for her future, build good relationships, feel good about herself and find her circle of support.
- A rite of passage celebration will allow your daughter to feel really special when puberty comes.

Teenagers are great people and you can have a terrific time parenting one! They are at a wonderfully interesting stage of their lives, and I have an optimistic view of parents' and teachers' ability to guide them through. These fickle and often exasperating young people really can transform into the visionaries and creators of an inspiring future. We are privileged to play a part in setting them on their path into that future. You are the expert where your child is concerned. You know her, you care for her and you want the best for her. I'd like to add my expertise to your unique role.

Becoming a woman is a marvel of transformation. Let's celebrate this transformation and make it a joyous one.

Guide to the book

The journey through this book follows the way in which our daughters grow up.

Part I, *Your preteen and the approach of puberty*, focuses on the initial phases of a girl's transition towards womanhood as puberty appears on her horizon. She is noticing how teen girls are and figuring out what it is to be a woman. At this stage, her concerns tend towards the impending physical changes her body will undergo.

Part II gets into *The chaos of adolescence*! So much is happening at this crucial time when rapid physical changes combine with heightened emotional sensitivity, new social interactions and big philosophical questions. We have a defining role in bringing forth the young adult by supporting girls to tackle their evolutionary job of figuring out who they are.

Part III, *Building her tribe of support, including her self*, discusses how teens can be guided safely through adolescence by nourishing their belief in themselves, by strengthening their 'tribe' and by celebrating their growing up.

Finally, there are certain sections that stand out from the main body of the book:

Girl Talk sections provide practical information written in language that your daughter can read. My hope is that you will use them to find the words to explain things to her. Alternatively, you can read them together, or you can allow her to read them on her own while letting her know that you are available to chat and answer questions. They are indicated by this picture:

There are four Girl Talk sections in the book:

Girl Talk – Puberty explained

Girl Talk – A girl's guide to periods

Girl Talk – About relationships

Girl Talk – How to lift your spirits

Case studies from my work. These sometimes merge girls' stories into one. Names have been changed throughout.

Key messages: over the years I have identified key ideas that seem central to the parenting of our girls. I have chosen to highlight these in bold italic to emphasise their importance.

Additional information can be found on www.ritesforgirls.com where you can learn more about Girls Journeying Together, Rites for Girls Facilitator Training, and coaching on creating your daughter's own rite of passage. You will also find my blog and useful links and resources there.

Growing up to fulfil her potential is every girl's right. We women can help. We know the powerful forces that can inhibit us from realising our dreams and we can work together to make the way easier for our daughters. We will heal through this engagement and we will all emerge stronger, more deeply connected and freer, becoming the wise women that the world needs. By supporting our girls with a loving, guiding and gently firm hand, we help to shape a better future for them, for society, and for our world.

PART I

Your preteen and
the approach of puberty

CHAPTER ONE

Starting with you

In this chapter, I discuss the concept of Mother–Daughter Dates, which can be introduced during the preteen years and continued right through adolescence. This powerful tool responds to our children's need to spend special time with us, as well as facilitating the natural process of guidance passing from mother to daughter. Mother–Daughter dates have proven to be highly effective even when relationships are strained.

YOUR CHILDREN NEED YOUR TIME

Teens, like toddlers, need parents to be around, involved, watchful and available. The teen years are a time of great vulnerability, growing self-awareness and increased anxiety. Adolescence brings greater freedom, exploration and experimentation, and these inevitably will lead to some poor decisions as well as a lot of good ones. There are many children who struggle. Some lose their way for a bit. It's hard to watch our children suffering or going in a direction that we wouldn't wish for them. A parent's impulse is to want to protect. It's not unusual to wish secretly that your child would go to sleep one night and wake in the morning as a young adult, leapfrogging the teen years altogether. You'd miss the defiance, the drunken mistakes, the rebellious choices, the regrettable dalliances, the late nights, the friends who seem anything but, the worry, and that feeling of losing control of your child, of losing your little girl.

If only there were a failsafe way of guaranteeing that our children will grow up okay ... Much as some parents might prefer to steer their child away from all potential risks and mistakes, the parent's task once their child approaches her teens is to allow her to make more of her own choices. Letting a toddler experience the biting chill of the wind when she insists on wearing a summer frock feels much easier than allowing a teen to experience the repercussions of wearing a crop top, miniskirt and heels when going out in the evening. Parenting a teenager can draw on all your reserves of patience, tolerance and courage. It can call for you to grow up yourself, to be 'the grown-up' in your interactions with her.

Parents have a delicate balance to find, knowing when to step back and when to step in; supporting our children's choices whenever possible and guiding them towards good ones. But the extent to which your child allows you to stay involved as she strikes out for more independence will depend on you maintaining a respectful relationship. I don't want parents to dread the teen years. They can be very rewarding, especially if you can give your children the priority and time that is required.

SHE IS WATCHING YOU . . .

Girls gather a sense of what is expected of womanhood from their mother, grandmothers, sisters, teachers, other women, peer group, older girls, films, television, advertisements, books, magazines, websites, computer games and social media. Watch your daughter trying to answer the question 'How does a girl become a woman?' with changes in the way she dresses and behaves, in what she says, and in what seems important to her. If you don't help your daughter to answer this question, others surely will. Some of her guiding influences will be good ones – but not all of them – and, whether you like it or not, you are probably her main guide to womanhood.

Can you remember when you were a girl watching your mother and making decisions about your life based on how you saw hers to be? Your daughter is going to have strong opinions about how she definitely does not want to be like you! She will be less aware of all the ways she does want her life to be like yours. You are her benchmark. Later on we will think about the importance of fathers and other males in your daughter's life, and also the importance of her having a circle of female support, but let's start by thinking about a mother's role in parenting her daughter safely through her teens. How you live your life is one of your greatest sources of influence. You are a woman, she is a girl going to be a woman, so she watches you, how you live, how you are with other people, what matters to you, and the choices that you make; and that defines womanhood for her. There will be other women who are important to her, but you are a key one. So, when your daughter looks at you, does life as a woman look appealing? Would she wish for a life like yours?

When I pose the question, 'What looks good about becoming a woman?' to the girls who come to Girls Journeying Together, a clamour of voices all proclaim the wonderful freedoms they perceive us women to have. From the girls' perspective, it seems that we can do whatever we choose, go wherever we want and stay out as late as we wish, eat what we want and go to bed when we feel like it. We can travel, earn money and spend it however we please. We can live where we want, wear what we like, and don't have exams or school. It all sounds terribly appealing and tells us a lot about their experience of the restrictions of childhood.

Then comes talk of family, children, careers. Still good, still positive. Eventually someone will say the word 'responsibility' and the conversation turns to bill paying, job worries, family concerns, marriage difficulties, feeding children, looking after pets and housework.

. . . .

Girls often perceive women's lives to be limited, burdened and boring. They fear that becoming a woman will mean having to give up on their dreams. We need to realise how we might be putting them off.

. . . .

Next, I ask the girls whether their own mothers are a good advert for womanhood – and things become pensive. This question gives some girls the opportunity to imagine themselves in their mothers' shoes –

something a self-focused teen may not do often. It's heart-warming to see.

'It feels like she's ruining my life, but she's just trying to look after me.'

'I hope I'm never like her – she worries about every little thing, but then I guess someone has to.'

When I ask mothers of teens, 'Are you a good advert for womanhood?' their responses can be sobering:

'I don't think I do make it look good at all. I'm always complaining about how much I've got to do and how little help I get. I hope she can also see how wonderful it is to have a family . . . and a job I mostly like.'

'I've stopped looking after myself enough – to her it must seem like my life is all about caring for other people. The other day she even said that I never did anything for myself. It was said like a criticism, but now I wonder if my life seems frightening to her; that hers might become that way too.'

. . . .

Allow yourself to make your life better and show your daughter an adult life to look forward to.

. . . .

We don't choose every aspect of our lives and we cannot control it all either, but we have a lot more choice and influence than we often allow ourselves. You are *not* powerless in the face of a troubling world for your daughter to grow up into. You have great power over how she rises to the challenge of growing up sure and strong. You can provide her with a role model in yourself and the women you surround her with.

You need to be willing to:

- Teach her how to self-care by taking care of yourself.
- Do whatever it takes to 'grow up' – even as adults we have areas of our personality or our behaviour that need attention so that we can parent with maturity.

- Slow down your life in order to have leisurely time with your daughter.
- Have the courage to talk about the awkward stuff even if your mum didn't.

If you could think of one thing to stop doing and one thing to start doing that would make your life better, what would these be? A small change can make a big difference...

MOTHER–DAUGHTER DATES

Parenting has brought out the very best in me and, I have to confess, at times the very worst. On bad days I reassure myself that no child wants the burden of a perfect parent! On good days, I feel like having children is the best thing imaginable and I delight in it.

I am a busy mum. I like the bustle of family life even when it's chaotic. My home is often dusty and messy and I wish it wasn't – but not enough to give up precious spare time to make it not so. Sometimes I feel as if my whole life revolves around my children, feeding them (meals come around so often!), ferrying them about (oh, for better public transport!), tidying up after them (or spending just as much time getting them to tidy up after themselves), tending to them (their needs really are endless) – but equally my life has never felt so meaningful and satisfying. Despite the many hours I spend in my children's company, in all this busyness I have to pay attention to avoid neglecting them. They are all well cared for, but if I'm not careful I can spend so much time cooking, shopping, driving, washing, doing for them that I don't make time for just relaxing with them. We think we spend plenty of time listening to our children, but there is something special that happens when a child feels that time has been set aside just for her.

The idea of a Mother–Daughter Date is for you to spend time alone together, once a month, for a few hours – just you and your daughter. The point is to be together, regularly: a 'date' she can count on. It can be a time to have fun, to really talk, to share a simple pleasure, to do something you have both been longing to do. Be as creative, simple, adventurous, ordinary, inexpensive, extravagant, experimental as you like. Ink it into the family diary. Once she realises that you plan to have this time together, she feels your commitment to her and it boosts her esteem. She knows that you want to create a regular special space for the two of you. Think about prioritising a Mother–Daughter Date over dance class, telly time, vacuuming or homework. If you think that you really cannot find a couple of hours once a month to spend with your daughter in this way, then perhaps this shows an imbalance in your lives . . .

In her preteen years

Mother–Daughter Dates can form the basis of a healthy and ongoing relationship with your daughter as she approaches puberty. Adolescence is a magical time, a phase of rapid change and a time when your daughter needs you close. She is probably beginning to spend less time with you and more with her friends. This might coincide with you working away from the home more. You will notice other changes: she seems to be growing up before your eyes; one minute she is playing with her dollies and the next she is experimenting with your eyeliner. You catch her dolefully eyeing herself in the mirror, angsting that she is fat – and her girlfriends seem to have so much sway over what she wants.

Even if things seem fine, this is the time to establish a way of staying connected. The closeness you shared when she was little changes, but it doesn't have to mean that you lose touch with each other.

Stop off on the way home for a hot chocolate. Go roller skating, to a film, to choose some seeds to plant. Walk the dog together at midnight. Watch her favourite programme with her. Sit and listen to each other's top tunes (without judgement). Experiment with making different flavours of popcorn. Colour in adjoining pages of an intricate colouring book. Let her do your hair. For inspiration, think back through your memories of precious times spent with adults when you were a child.

When you develop a regular Mother–Daughter Date routine while your child is growing up you give her a habit of expecting to spend special time together that she will want to hang on to into her teens. You co-create a space to enjoy each other's company, even when friends become more important, even during tense times, especially when she needs you but feels like she ought to manage on her own.

Even though the idea of having a Mother–Daughter Date is simple, many mothers report amazing developments in their relationship with their daughters as a direct result. Try it.

Sophia is reminded that her mother is always there for her

Cathy and her daughter Sophia had always been close. Sophia told her mother everything – in great detail and at length! Cathy heard all about what went on at school, who was getting on with who, what Sophia wanted to spend her birthday money on, all about the characters in her favourite TV programmes, her changing music tastes, and her hopes for the future ... Just recently, though, since Sophia started at secondary school, she didn't seem so keen to share so much with her mum. Cathy knew this might be normal but still missed the closeness they had. She sensed that maybe something was troubling her daughter, but when asked Sophia just said that she was fine. In the end Cathy took her daughter away for a day by the sea, leaving her brother and dad at home. They played mini-golf, paddled and ate ice cream. In the evening, over fish and chips, Sophia started to talk about herself – her worries about making the grade at school, complications in new friendships, feeling like she ought not to need her mum so much, feeling really moody for no reason, moody with her mum sometimes too. Sophia felt her mother's support that day and, although she still shared less with her, she was reminded that she always could and that it helped. Cathy made a point of making time to be alone with her daughter every few weeks.

Mother–Daughter Dates give extra support at that time in the month

Mel was a single, hard-working mother who worked shifts to be able to be at home when her two daughters got in from school. As soon as the girls arrived home, the three of them had a family routine of walking the dog together. When Ella, her eldest, started her periods, Mel changed the routine a bit – on the first day of her period Ella often didn't feel like walking, so Mel would go with her youngest, leaving Ella at home on the sofa with a hot water bottle. The following day she and Ella would go alone and stop off at the local café on their way back, a nice treat for Ella. This casual habit became really important – Ella knew that she would have time alone with her mother right at the time of the month when she was often full of complicated feelings and needed to talk. It was something she could rely on.

And on, into her teens

Whether or not you have established a regular routine of having Mother–Daughter Dates through her pre–teen years, the teen years are the time to make sure you have regular special time with her. You might find that:

- You love aspects of watching her grow up, but you worry that it's happening too fast.
- You feel your daughter takes too much notice of her friends' opinions.
- You want your daughter's adolescence to be easier than yours.
- Something is troubling her, but she won't tell you what.

- You want to make her feel special when she starts menstruating, but you don't want to embarrass her.
- You feel like you are losing her.
- Every morning you promise yourself that you won't lock horns with your daughter, but you still do.

Take her to your favourite café, a good film, on a country walk, to your childhood home, go swimming, get your nails done, redesign her bedroom, sky-dive . . . Tell her about what you admire in her, about your dreams as a teenager, about your mother, about your aspirations for yourself now. Ask her about her dreams and aspirations. Above all, listen to her. Listen without judging or guiding her.

Let your teen know that she can rely on you to spend special time with her every month, whatever else is going on. Stick to your Mother–Daughter Date even when the emotional climate is difficult between you and the last thing you feel like doing is spending time together. Make it an unquestioned habit that is never denied as a consequence of bad behaviour – honour your date even when you feel she doesn't deserve it. Finally, keep it going even if you have already had lots of time together that month, or if life feels so busy that it seems impossible to find time.

Time your Mother–Daughter Dates to coincide with the week that she is menstruating. We all know that feelings can be heightened around this time of the month, so the treat of time alone together can become a valuable pressure-release valve where you can give her the opportunity to talk, sound off, weep, take a break and feel your support. Arranging your special meeting at this time of the month can also become a private but powerful acknowledgement between you of her status – that of a developing young woman.

This is deceptively simple and yet very powerful. Everything that is precious about your relationship will show itself here. Everything that is hard about your relationship will also surface. No matter what, keep the Mother–Daughter Dates commitment going.

Small steps to get back in touch

By the time Ava was thirteen she was already following in her older sister's footsteps, barely home and hanging out with her friends after school and at weekends. They weren't a bad crowd, but Ava's mum felt they had too much influence over her. Her grades were slipping and she'd given up the after-school swimming club that she used to love. Ava and her mother weren't getting on at all. When I suggested regular Mother–Daughter Dates, Ava's mum could not imagine her daughter ever wanting to do anything with her. So she started small – she bought some fancy biscuits and joined her on the sofa while Ava was watching her favourite show. Even though Ava's mum hated the show, she could see that sharing treats and the weekly storyline with her daughter was giving them both something precious.

Ella gets the attention she needs

Ella was a happy child, studious, popular and busy. If something was going on, she would be involved. The eldest of three, she could be relied on to be helpful at home, which was good as her dad travelled for work and her mum worked part-time and helped to run the local Girl Guides unit. Life looked good for the family. That was until Ella fainted at school, for a second time, and although she insisted that she felt fine, her mother decided to take her for a check-up with the doctor. The doctor could find nothing wrong but asked that they return if Ella fainted again. Two weeks later they were back – and the doctor was shocked to see the change in Ella. She was losing weight. Tests quickly ruled out a number of possible causes. Ella kept saying she was fine and this alerted the doctor to what lay behind it all – Ella was starving herself. She was anorexic but had managed to hide this until now. She skipped meals and moved her food around on the plate rather than eating it. Her family tried everything: tempting her with favourite foods, making her stay at the table until she had finished, rewarding her with extra pocket money for eating, removing privileges if she didn't. Sadly, Ella's condition worsened and she was hospitalised a couple of times. She was also given someone to talk to – a play therapist – and slowly she began to speak about the feelings that she felt unable to express at home. Gradually she began to gain weight. Her mother, always anxious to do whatever she could to help her daughter, trawled the internet for guidance. She came across the idea of Mother–Daughter Dates and began to take Ella out once a week without her siblings. At first it felt awkward: they'd not spent time alone together and it felt artificial and forced. Ella's mother kept at it, each week thinking up somewhere new to go together, even though none of her ideas seemed to make it more comfortable. And then one week she took Ella to a cat rescue centre and over a box of scrawny orphan kittens it all poured out – how Ella wasn't happy but didn't know why and hadn't wanted to bother her parents because they were so busy and anyway she felt she had no good reason to feel down. Ella's journey of recovery took many months, but her weekly trip to the cat rescue centre with her mother played an important part in her figuring out how to feel better.

WHAT IF A MOTHER–DAUGHTER DATE FEELS IMPOSSIBLE?

Is her behaviour at home becoming unreasonable, unrecognisable and intolerable?

Do you ever ask yourself, 'Who is this person?' or, 'Where has my lovely little girl gone?'

Does your daughter seem more concerned about her friends, her appearance and her social media than about being on good terms with you?

If any or all of these things are the case, then somewhere along the line you have stopped being her relied-upon support, her trusted advocate, her sympathetic ear and shoulder to cry on. If her peers have taken over this role then you need to reassert yourself – not as her best friend, but as the best parent you can be. Her peers are not the best people to guide your daughter through to adulthood. They are on that same journey, and teenage relationships can be volatile, fickle and brutal – as well as fun, supportive and empowering. You truly are her best bet. Be a parent who she feels is on her side, who seeks to understand her point of view, but who is also able to be firm, reasonable and committed. Teenagers feel safest when their parents are actively involved in their lives, even when they are baulking at your restrictions and cursing your demands on them.

Sometimes disrespect, poor communication and bad behaviour lead to a breakdown of the mother–daughter relationship, preventing you from being a good parent to her. In order to re-establish a close relationship with your daughter, why not try going away together for a few days? Just the two of you. Treat her, take her out of school even. Leave your work and any other commitments behind, no matter how hard this may be to organise. The message you want to give is that your daughter and your relationship with her are more important.

Be creative. Do whatever it takes to reconnect. You know your daughter really well; trust that you do, and you can find your way back to her. Initially you will need to take her away from home ground and from her friends – and give it time. While you are away, create situations where she needs to rely on you again, for example by doing something that requires cooperation. Examples of mother–daughter adventures that have been successful are canoeing, a cookery course, a trip abroad, walking home from some unknown destination, making a film of childhood haunts, and youth hostelling. Give her opportunities to take full responsibility, for example by preparing a meal of her choice, map-reading, making a photo-journal of your time or even planning your whole day. Having a few days away is just the start. On your return, make a date each month to spend time together. This will maintain your new connection and build on what you have started.

If you find that you are in the habit of feeling irritated by your teen, not approving of her, or even disliking her, think about how changing your perspective might help. She has to feel that you are on her side for her to let you guide her. To dare to trust you with her worries and her mistakes, she needs to feel that you believe in her and that you won't always assume the worst. This may require a huge leap of faith on your part, but try to remember how you felt at her age. Teenagers are vulnerable. They want their parents' approval, even if they seem not to. They want to have friends and to be liked. They want to have control over their own lives and to feel that they are grown-up enough to be given that freedom.

When a child behaves 'badly' it can help to look at this as her attempt to solve a problem. Look beyond her actions to discover what is really important to her – more important than your good opinion. Take your clues from the challenging behaviour. A child who becomes withdrawn and rude may be suffering from being bullied. A teen who turns to alcohol or other drugs may be trying to numb feelings she can't deal with. A person who seems obsessed by her appearance may be feeling insecure about who she is.

Just because you are mother and daughter is no guarantee that you will like each other and get on – but know that both of you want to, however difficult it may seem. Check that you are giving what is needed for you and your daughter to have a good relationship. You can help by focusing on the good in your daughter's behaviour and casually remarking on it. Find support from other parents who won't judge your daughter but will help you to find compassion for her. When talking about your daughter bear in mind the sensitivity and self-consciousness of teenagers, select carefully who you confide in and speak about her respectfully, or you risk losing her trust in you.

Casey's mum finds a way to get close again

Casey was caught shoplifting. It was the last straw for her mother, Joan – she knew she had to do something but she didn't know what. Casey was rude and lazy and was treating home like a hotel. She was hanging out with a bad crowd and Joan knew that she'd been lying to her about a boyfriend. Joan suspected Casey had filched money from her purse, too. Home life was miserable: just one row after another followed by sulky silences. Joan turned to her sister for help, and her sister offered them her house for a long weekend while she was away on holiday. Joan wasn't even sure she'd be able to get Casey to come. Missing a day of school turned out to be a good enough incentive. When they arrived there, they found an envelope with cash and a note: 'Please turn Amy's bedroom into a "big girl's room". Here's the money to do it.' They didn't get off to a good start, with arguments at the DIY shop, Joan trying to curb Casey's extravagant ideas, and Casey insisting that her mother take her back home. Hot chocolate and watching a comedy together changed the mood. The next morning, Joan handed over control to Casey, warning her to stay within budget so that they wouldn't leave the job half-done. Casey impressed her mother with how she tackled it all, really thinking about what her cousin Amy would like, and finding innovative ways of making her room really special. But when it came to calculating how much paint would be needed, Casey was out of her depth and had to turn to her mum for help. It wasn't without hitches, but mostly they spent a companionable few days transforming the room and shared in the glow of Amy's excitement when she returned. On the drive back home, Joan suggested that they give Casey's room a make-over together, and this was the beginning of a number of shared projects that kept their new-found amicableness going. Joan learned not to criticise the choices that Casey was making, and gradually Casey began to ask her advice again.

BECOMING A WOMAN IS A PROCESS

Transforming from a girl to a woman is a journey. Some girls appear to hurtle towards womanhood at an alarming pace; others are more reluctant. Too often their peers seem to be their main support during this phase, sometimes behaving like partners in crime rather than true allies. *You* need to guide your daughter safely and healthily from childhood, through puberty and towards womanhood.

Essential to the healthy development of our teens is to teach them womanly things, and this happens over time, not just in one discussion. Conversations about C cups, growing pubic hair or romance don't emerge out of thin air. A climate of trust and easy communication must exist between a girl and a woman before the sensitive topics can be broached. This evolves over time and requires a conscious effort on the woman's part to pay attention to the girl's life and have a wish to tiptoe into her world. At a time when our girls may give off the impression that they need us less, they just need us differently. Puberty is a time of many changes, and, welcome or not, it's going to be somewhat unnerving.

No matter how happy you imagine your daughter's life to be, how stable her family, or how supportive her friends, do not assume that she can always handle the intensity of teenage emotions. Build a relationship with her that gives you regular opportunities for making time to talk by stepping out of everyday life. Listen to her, really listen. And if you are going through a patch when closeness is tricky, persist. Keep looking for ways of spending fun time together, and make sure that you are not the only woman in her life who cares. Build a circle of women who are actively involved in her life and who she can turn to if you are not the right support at any time, or if for some reason you can't be available.

Don't rely only on playground chatter, social and relationship education at school, music videos or social media to teach your daughter about how to become a woman. Find the courage to broach the awkward issues yourself. Plan monthly Mother–Daughter Dates and choose activities to share that will give you and your daughter opportunities to talk intimately.

Being a good parent to a teen is mostly about being a good person – living in a way that you would want her to live. Look after yourself and aim to have the most agreeable life you can have. Do your best, and then forgive yourself for your weaknesses. Treat your daughter well. Allow her to be whoever she is. And commit to regular time together.

CHAPTER TWO

Preparing your daughter for puberty

The act of parenting can bring great healing to mothers (and fathers) as we revisit our own memories of childhood and adolescence. Many of us remember our experience of puberty acutely. When you think back to how your mother approached your puberty, can you remember how you felt? You can copy what she did that was good, and plan how you will improve on it for your daughter.

There are two key aspects to making these pivotal years special. On the one hand, you need to prepare yourself and have the courage to speak about womanly things. You cannot take your daughter where you are not yet comfortable yourself. On the other hand, you will need to familiarise yourself with the practical information that you need to pass onto her. In this chapter, we will cover both concerns so that you can help to make puberty a magical time for your daughter. In Girl Talk you have explanations that you can use, and there are case studies from my practice that show examples of how to move forward if you feel apprehensive about what is coming.

PREPARE YOURSELF

If your daughter is eight (yes, eight!), then puberty might be just around the corner. Have you prepared her? Puberty for girls in 'developed' countries normally starts at between eight and thirteen years old. This means that we must begin preparing our girls by age seven. You also need to give time to your own personal development so that you won't hinder your ability to guide your daughter towards healthy adulthood. Ask yourself big questions such as these:

What does it mean to live a meaningful and fulfilling life?

What are my morals and values?

What more could I do to have a meaningful and fulfilling life, living according to these morals and values?

How might I resolve any unfinished business from my childhood?

What still needs attention in my life for me to be the best version of myself?

Answering these questions may be done in quiet contemplation, a lively debate with friends or a heart-to-heart with someone close, or with the help of a counsellor.

FIND THE COURAGE TO SPEAK

Many mothers want to be the go-to person when their daughter needs guidance at puberty, but often they feel awkward and don't know what to say. Many women didn't have their mothers prepare them well for puberty, so they don't have a good example to follow. Don't be discouraged – you are still one of the best qualified to tell your child about the changes that lie ahead and help her to explore who she wants to become.

Find the courage to speak to your daughter about periods, sex, dreams and life purpose. Some mothers find these things easy to chat about, but others don't. Be brave! The world offers many opportunities to bring these topics into your conversation through what happens to people around you or in the media. Be aware of opportunities for conversations to arise naturally – in the bathroom, while you are dressing, at birthdays or New Year, or when on a Mother–Daughter Date. Listen to your daughter; try to understand her and hold back from preaching. You could break the ice by telling her how you learned about puberty and explain how you want it to be for her. Personal stories are a great way of talking about these things: they are powerful and memorable. It's the way mothers have been teaching their daughters since the dawn of time.

Practise talking about puberty with your friends so that you become more comfortable with finding the words. Don't rely on school or her peers to help your daughter explore the important issues of adolescence such as peer pressure, cultural influences, managing stress, mood swings, body image, sex, drugs, education, dreams and plans, personal heritage, values, how to manage money, creative ways of self-expression, giving back, health, fitness, good eating and self-care.

Your daughter probably wants to know about these things before you feel ready for her to want to know about them! In the following pages I'll cover the most often asked questions and concerns of the preteens in my Girls Journeying Together groups. Some girls want to know what lies ahead, and talking about it before puberty arrives helps them to welcome the changes rather than fear them. Others don't feel ready for puberty or for talking about it. Make sure your daughter has the information for when she does want it, and let her know you are happy to talk when she feels ready.

Briony wants her daughters to be better informed than she was

When Briony was growing up, her mother didn't tell her anything about what to expect – it just wasn't spoken about. Briony has two daughters and she wants it to be different for them, but she can't quite bring herself to talk to them openly about personal things. She confessed this to a good friend, who invited her along to her church circle, and there Briony was shocked to find herself among women who talked candidly about their husbands, their children, their disappointments and their dreams. Over time, she began to find herself able to speak more openly too. It turned out that she wasn't the only one worried about how to explain puberty to her girls. By talking with other mothers about how they all wanted to do it differently from when they were young, Briony found the words for how to broach it with her daughters.

Emily found television helped her to speak openly with her daughter

It happened by accident – Emily's daughter was recovering from a bad bout of flu and was feeling miserable. Emily rearranged her shifts so that she could stay home with her daughter, and they snuggled on the sofa together watching daytime TV. A chat show on teen pregnancy sparked a giggling conversation that began with discussing morning sickness and ended with flavoured condoms!

Deciding when to have 'The Sex Talk'

Never have just one 'talk'. Better to have a conversation that starts in the toddler years and spans your daughter's entire childhood and into her teens. It's never too late: begin a discussion whenever the topic arises naturally. This way she knows that you're happy to talk about bodies and babies and that she can come to you with her questions. It's not possible to predict what your child will need to know, or when, so be guided by what she asks. I tend to err on the side of saying less and pausing to see if this prompts further enquiry. In that way I'm not telling her more than she is ready to hear.

Some parents worry that talking about sex will encourage their child to try things sooner. In fact research indicates that talking to children about sexual matters is positively related to *delaying* their first sexual experience;[1] and it's a conversation that is so much more comfortable for everyone if started in your child's early years. Covering the basics before she starts school is your best defence against misinformation that may come from peers or elsewhere. I am surprised by how little some girls know. They tell me that when it's covered in school it's too awkward to really take it in and it's definitely not comfortable to ask questions. Many go online to find out. Make sure your daughter knows everything that she needs to.

PREPARING YOUR DAUGHTER – THE PRACTICAL STUFF

When do you start? Now!

How do you do it? Spend time alone with your daughter, whatever her age. Encourage her interests (even if they are not your own), make her aware of her strengths, invite her questions, discuss womanly things, teach her how to take care of herself, and have fun together.

Who can help? The women in her life – you, her grandmother, aunts, cousins, older sisters, godmother, family friends, friends' mothers, a favourite teacher. Ask yourself who she can open her heart to and ensure that she can spend time with this person. Hopefully there are important males in your daughter's life too, and their role is covered in a later chapter.

Cover the practical stuff. Much of this is in the Girl Talk section at the end of this chapter, and the rest is addressed later in the book.

---

1 NHS Centre for Reviews and Dissemination, 'Preventing and reducing the adverse effects of unintended teenage pregnancies', *Effective Healthcare Bulletin* 3(1), University of York (1997),

Show her the fun things about being a woman. Open the door into your woman's world and invite your daughter in. Share girly nights, snuggle on the sofa with a film, eat out, host a clothes-swap evening, pass on a favourite read, share cinnamon toast late at night, go shopping somewhere unusual, feed the ducks, have a brew and a chat, splash out on a spa session, buy luxury chocolates, hike in the woods, have a pyjama day.

Help her feel good about her changing body. Focus on how her body feels rather than what it looks like. Being healthy feels good; have wholesome food in the house, avoid creating a culture of dieting, run her a fragrant candlelit bath, get enough sleep. Be physically active. Help her to find clothes she feels good in (even if they are not what you'd choose). Ban yourself from making any negative comments about her physical appearance (or yours).

Encourage her to express herself. Give her a lockable diary, sketch pad, lump of clay, voice recorder.

Stay deeply involved and make moments to remember. Many pubescent girls give the impression of wanting less parental involvement in their lives. Don't be fooled! You are needed at this time more than ever before. Give her space but make sure she has your attention too. Make moments to remember. Create opportunities for her to prove to herself and to others that she is indeed successfully on her way to becoming her own woman.

Discuss how she would like you to acknowledge her growing up. Talk with your daughter about how your responsibility for her will ebb as her responsibility for herself grows. There will be times when she will need to prove her readiness to take on more; other times when you will need to let go and allow her independence. A rite-of-passage ceremony can help you both along the way.

Take on the role of preparing your daughter for her first bleed and consider some way of marking this. Creating a puberty ritual is a powerful way of asking her to step into greater maturity and at the same time help you to let go. Read about how to create one in the final chapter of this book.

Girl Talk – Puberty explained

What is happening to me?

Puberty brings changes in your body, your feelings and your thoughts. Some girls can't wait for it to happen; others aren't so sure and don't feel ready yet. It's normal to feel excited and daunted, curious and nervous.

Puberty for girls normally starts between eight and thirteen years old and is finished by age sixteen or seventeen. You can't slow it down or hurry it along.

Here are some of the physical changes to expect:

- A growth spurt happens, especially legs, arms, hands and feet.
- Face lengthens and voice deepens a little.
- Body sweats more.
- Skin and hair become more oily – you may have spots.
- Arms and legs become hairier.
- Soft hair grows under arms and between legs, which later becomes thicker and curly.
- Nipples grow, darken and become tender.
- Breasts grow – sometimes one before the other.
- Body gains weight, changes shape and becomes more curvaceous; hips widen.
- Vaginal discharge – a small amount of sticky, whitish fluid in your knickers.
- Vulva and labia (between your legs) increase in size.
- Your period starts, eventually settling into a regular monthly pattern.

Some of the changes happen to prepare your body to be able to have children one day if you want to. Becoming a woman is not just about being able to have babies: it's also about gaining the freedom to make choices about what you want to do, who you want to be with, where you want to live, how you want to spend your money, and what is important to you. You will also be taking charge of what you eat and when you go to bed!

As you mature you can enjoy new freedoms, but with those come greater responsibilities. Your parents will find it easier to loosen their control if you show that you'll take good care of yourself (most of the time at least).

This is a time of letting go. Your parents are letting go as they figure out how to hand over to you the running of your life. You are letting go of some of the comforts and conveniences of being a child as you take on caring for yourself more. It's quite all right to feel a bit sad about that, as well as excited. Free of some childhood restrictions, you will get to know yourself better as you take charge of your life.

What do you need to know?

Many girls find the changes that lie ahead a bit daunting. Who looks forward to greasy hair, smelly armpits, spots, and hair in new places? Not everyone welcomes bras and monthly bleeding. But the spots pass, you find a favourite deodorant, and you get used to the new hair; there are some lovely bras to choose from, most of the changes in puberty settle down, and you get used to your monthly bleed. Teething and learning to walk might have seemed troublesome when you were a baby, but it was worth it for the increased freedom. It's a similar situation now.

Feelings change during adolescence too. Many girls find that they feel things more strongly – they rage and weep and worry more easily. Feelings towards parents change and mature. Your whole being is preparing you to be able to speak up for what you believe in, do what feels right for you, live how you want and feel like a woman.

Here are some things to know about:

Body odour

You will need to wash more often than you did when you were younger. Fresh sweat smells fine, but old sweat has a strong smell that you may not be aware of on yourself.

Bathe or shower regularly, and on days when you don't, flannel wash the hairy bits.

Wear fresh, clean clothes. If they're made of natural, breathable fibres (cotton, viscose, silk, wool), you will sweat less.

Drink more water – your sweat will smell less.

Experiment with different deodorants. Take note of the ingredients, as some are better for you than others. Be aware that antiperspirants often contain toxins and stop your body from sweating, which isn't healthy.

Acne

Spots! Just when you're becoming more self-conscious about how you look, your face erupts into pimples. Spots are pores clogged by the extra oil your skin produces during puberty. How many spots you have is partly down to hormones, partly genes and partly lifestyle. The lifestyle part is where you have some control over your spots.

You may not want to hear this, but if you can drink more water, and cut back on fatty, oily foods, sweets and processed foods, you will see a big improvement in your skin. Getting enough sleep also helps.

For clear skin, keep it clean. Wash your face every morning and night and after exercise, rubbing gently with a warm, wet flannel. Avoid soap and astringent spot cleansers, as they dry your skin out and encourage it to produce more oil. If a spot becomes red and infected, dab a little witch hazel, tea tree oil or lavender oil (all natural antiseptics) on it. Avoid make-up that covers pores. Above all, resist the urge to squeeze your spots – this will stimulate oilier skin and open the skin up to infection; the spot gets bigger and redder, and it can leave a scar.

If none of this works and you have really bad acne, check with your doctor.

Greasy hair

Switch to a shampoo for greasier hair, but don't wash your hair too often. Daily washing strips your hair of its natural oils and sends messages to produce more oil, making the problem worse.

Curves

Curves are feminine and are part of having a woman's body. The changes are in preparation for your childbearing years, so celebrate your body gaining some weight and some shape. Sadly, we live in a culture where skinny, girl-like bodies are in fashion, and many women learn to dislike and battle against their natural female shape, so you will need to find inner strength to love yours.

Exercising and eating well help you to feel good about your body.

During a growth spurt, you may experience 'growing pains' and stretch marks. Check with your doctor if these are very painful, but normally the pains will pass and the stretch marks will fade.

Breasts

Some of the best new curves you're going to get are breasts! When they come and how big they become is not something you can influence. Your left and right breast are unlikely to be exactly the same.

Some girls experience breast tenderness. This can be eased by taking daily evening primrose oil capsules for a few weeks. Wearing a crop top can stop your clothes from rubbing against tender nipples.

Bras

You will know that you need the support of a bra when your breasts feel uncomfortable when you run. Bras come in different sizes, which are shown by a number and a letter. The number is how wide you are around the rib cage (usually between 28 and 38 inches), and the letter is the breast size, or cup size (typically AA, A, B, C, D). It's important to wear the right size bra – although about 85 per cent of women don't! All good lingerie shops or department stores will have someone who can help you to find the right fit. They will measure you over your vest and then leave you to try different bras on in private.

Buying your first bra is a special moment. Think about who you would like to have with you.

Body hair

We live in a time and a culture where many women choose to remove some of the hair that grows on their bodies. It's your choice. Hair removal takes time and costs money, repeatedly, and can make you itchy and stubbly. However, if the fashion is to appear hairless in places, then you need self-confidence to choose not to remove yours. Many women shave, wax or epilate in the summer, bothering less in the winter.

Vaginal discharge and menstruation

You may notice a sticky whitish mark in your underwear, which may smell a bit musky. This means your period is likely to start about six to twelve months later. The smell is normal. Just wash daily with warm water – soap upsets your natural pH – and there's no need to wash inside, as your vagina cleans itself.

To understand more about the monthly cycle that is beginning in your body, read Girl Talk – A girl's guide to periods, in Chapter Three. Finding out what is happening during your cycle will allow you to predict when your bleeding days will be each month, and later on will help you to manage your fertility.

Physical self-exploration

Be curious to watch how your body changes. It's natural to find it both pleasing and alarming. Make friends with your 'new body' by spending time privately in front of a mirror, looking with kind eyes.

Puberty is a great time to get to know your body a bit better. Don't be afraid to explore yourself more closely. Find a private place to squat over a mirror and find your urethra (where you pee), your vagina (where you menstruate), and your clitoris (which feels really nice).

You may feel really conscious of your body as it's changing so much, but always remember that how you look is only one aspect of you. How you behave, what you think, how you express yourself, how you feel about things, what stirs your soul: these are also important aspects of you. If you think about your friends, do you like them for how they look, or for how they are?

Sex

It's natural to feel sexual and to become interested in romance as you grow older. When you are attracted to somebody, remember what you already know about finding good friends. Do you have stuff to talk about, are you kind to each other, can you trust this person with your secrets, do you feel safe in their company, do you get on, can you feel a connection? Romance means being close mentally, emotionally and spiritually as well as physically. And the physical part need only be as much as feels right to you. Listen to your instincts, and if ever you feel pressured then take that as a sign to step back a bit. Trust your own body to guide you in what to do in order to be physically close to someone, and avoid porn if you can, as it's a bad teacher for good sex. If anything doesn't feel right, stop. If your partner doesn't respect that, then they are not the right partner. Find someone wise and trustworthy to talk to if ever you feel unsure. Have fun!

Emotional changes

As you head towards your teens, you may find that your emotions intensify. Mood swings are stronger, with higher highs and lower lows and less time in between.

Many tweens and teens feel more:

- Self-conscious and easily embarrassed.
- Anxious.
- Irritable, frustrated, angry, and morning moody.
- Sensitive and likely to get offended.
- Tearful.

It will ease after a few years, but you're going to need to look after yourself in these emotional times. It may seem unlikely, but mood swings can be lessened by simple things like regular good sleep, exercise, healthy diet, time alone, and time with good friends and family.

A time of adventure

Even though puberty is a time of much change, you're still you – always. You may find yourself becoming more curious about who 'you' are. Teens often experiment with their style, dress, taste in music, friendships and approach to life. You may feel more adventurous and more likely to question the authority of adults, wishing to find out and decide things for yourself. Great – go ahead! And stay safe.

You are now in a phase of life when you need to take more responsibility for your own wellbeing. You might sometimes make poor choices – everyone does at any age – but taking care of yourself is very important. The adults in your life will find it much easier to hand over to you if they can see that you take your responsibilities seriously. Remember, parents really care and are usually trying to do what they believe is right for you.

A time of struggle

Some teens find it hard to make good choices and take good care of themselves. Talk to an adult you trust if you find yourself being too much influenced by friends who are making bad decisions about smoking, drugs, sex, drinking, stealing, bullying or something else. Find the courage to talk to a trusted adult if you are self-harming, not eating sensibly, becoming obsessive or hating yourself or your life. You're not alone – many teens struggle with these things. Don't try to cope on your own; there are many adults who have experience in helping young people with these problems.

A time of prejudice

Unfortunately, some people can seem prejudiced against teenagers, even teachers and loving parents. The prejudice can be subtle and often unquestioned. Teenagers often get a bad rap, accused of being moody, uncommunicative, unmotivated, impulsive, uncontrollable, rebellious, violent and disrespectful. Some teens do behave in these ways, but there's always an underlying reason, even if it isn't always obvious. Not having enough sleep is a surprisingly common cause of many of these behaviours. If you find yourself trapped in habitual antisocial behaviour, seek out a wise and trusted adult to talk to.

Prove them wrong – teens are great!

And one more thing . . .

Adolescence is a special time. Your body is changing, your feelings are fluctuating, your friendships are adjusting, and your outlook on life is evolving. This can be confusing, exciting, daunting and exhilarating by turns.

It's normal to find yourself feeling grown-up one day and like a child another. Your relationship with your parents shifts and you experience the world differently. What matters to you changes. Many teens discover new highs and new lows – feeling rubbish at times and over the moon at others. There are fantastic moments, and mistakes to learn from. You will mature and discover new things, gain new responsibility and earn new freedoms. Your friends can play an ever-important part in your life. A wise girl also has older friends and family to support her – people who care and have wisdom to share.

* *

Thousands of girls are on a similar journey right now and millions and millions of women have trodden the path before you. There is no right way to grow up, and you will find your own way.

* *

CHAPTER THREE

Periods – bloody nuisance or bleedin' miracle?

Starting her periods is one of the milestones in a girl's life. This chapter provides basic information on the first period, how to prepare your daughter well and help her to have a good monthly cycle, as well as managing any period problems. As always, I emphasise that the passing of information can be done in a special way that strengthens your relationship and teaches her about the age-old art of women supporting women. You can gift your daughter with a gentle preparation that starts early on in her childhood, long before she needs to know, and add more details as she matures. It's never too late to have these conversations, even if she is menstruating already. The Girl Talk section, A girl's guide to periods, provides information for your conversations with her.

Many women don't much like having a monthly bleed, and for some it can be a real ordeal. Lots of women think of their periods as being messy and inconvenient, and for many it brings pain and mood swings. How do we make all that sound appealing to a young girl on the brink of starting?

In my Girls Journeying Together groups I introduce girls to women who have a good experience of bleeding monthly. You *can* find them! Many women like the regular rhythm that a period brings to their lives and the fact that it signals their health and fertility. When I gather women to talk about their experiences of monthly bleeding, they also share with the girls tips for what can help with cramping and moodiness.

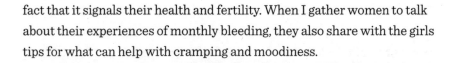

In the past women were thought powerful because we can bleed without dying; indeed, our bleeding indicates our ability to carry new life.

Every period can be a time of feeling that power.

BLEEDING FOR THE FIRST TIME

When your daughter bleeds for the first time, this heralds a significant change – she can now conceive, carry and bear a child. That's quite a collection of super-powers! She has taken a special step on her journey towards womanhood and joins an international sisterhood of all the girls and women around the world who are bleeding.

Our first bleed, also called menarche, is a threshold experience: in a single moment we pass through a gateway. Most women clearly remember their first time. How did you feel? What was special about the experience? How would you have liked it to be different? Who did you tell? How did they respond? How might your experience influence how you approach your daughter's first bleed?

A girl's experience of her first period comes at a time of great hormonal change and varies enormously from one girl to another. For some it is a long-awaited and welcome marker of a new and special status. For others it can be a dreaded and embarrassing event. Some feel quietly, privately special. Some feel overwhelmed and full of fear. Some struggle with mood swings, cramps and bloating. Others can't understand what all the fuss is about. For many girls it's an intensely private event and not something they would want to broadcast. You will need to respect your daughter's wish for privacy, even though you may be bursting with feelings.

A girl's first period is much easier if she has been well prepared. If you were able to talk to your daughter about your period while she was still young, she is more likely to welcome it when her time comes. It's a delicate subject to raise, but raise it we must, or risk our girls being uneducated, misinformed, ashamed, awkward and fearful – a potentially harmful cocktail. The listening helpline Samaritans was set up in 1953 in response to the suicide of a fourteen-year-old girl who started her periods and, having no one to talk to, believed that she had an embarrassing disease.

If nobody ever talked to you reassuringly about periods when you were growing up then it's normal for you to find it awkward. Help is at hand! You can use Girl Talk – A girl's guide to periods, in this chapter. When periods are mentioned on television or in other media, seize the moment and talk about them. Find a book. Use humour. Have a giggle. If you have been having Mother–Daughter Dates this can happen more easily because you have created a private space and a climate of intimacy together. If you resort to giving your daughter a book, read it first and find a way to talk about it after she has had a chance to look at it. And if you are just too uneasy talking about periods with her, find someone else who can. Think of a woman in your family or circle of friends who might be willing to take that role in your daughter's life. Ask her auntie or your daughter's best friend's mother. Some girls prefer to hear it from someone a bit removed from their everyday life; just don't leave it up to her peer group – this is your turf, not theirs.

Make her a keepsake memory

When your daughter starts to bleed, or when she tells you that she has started, mark the specialness of the event – but tread carefully: you are on sacred ground and your daughter requires sensitivity and respect.

Here are some ways in which mothers have honoured their daughter's first bleed:

- A heart-shaped lavender bag on her pillow.
- Chocolates 'not for sharing'.

- A much longed-for trip to have her ears pierced.
- A heartfelt letter.
- A long walk somewhere unusual.
- Red flowers on her bedside table.
- A family meal out.
- A spontaneous wild swim.
- A new-style haircut.
- Planting a tree.
- Fancy new underwear.
- A road trip.

This may also feel like the right time to create a rite-of-passage ceremony to mark her coming of age (see Chapter Nine).

A girl's menarche is something to be honoured and celebrated. Hopefully one day our culture will become more accepting of what girls and women need in order to enjoy their monthly cycle, and all girls will have a sense of pride in their period rather than carrying embarrassment throughout their lives.

Other mothers can make the period talk easier

Sarah's mum had left a leaflet about periods on Sarah's bed, so she had no idea how to prepare her own daughter Emily. She asked Emily's best friend's mum, who invited them over to watch a coming-of-age film and, as they all giggled over a shared pizza afterwards, the conversation naturally turned to puberty. Sarah found that she could talk about it after all.

Lucy's mum made it easier by talking openly right from the start

Lucy first found out about periods when she was about five and noticed a blood stain on her mother's clothing. 'Oh, yes, it's my bleeding time,' her mother had explained, and Lucy hadn't thought much of it. A short while later she asked her mother if it hurt. 'No, this is special blood. It's not like when you cut yourself. This is blood that comes once a month when you are a woman.' About a year later Lucy wanted to understand more and they talked about where the blood came from and why. She'd seen her mother's pads and tampons in the bathroom and now she knew what they were for. By the time she started her own periods Lucy knew what to expect and how to manage it. She taught a few of her friends too!

Hayley was an early starter and no one was prepared

Gemma was shocked to find a plastic bag full of blood-soiled knickers under her daughter Hayley's bed. Hayley was only ten. Too young. It hadn't occurred to Gemma that they were anywhere near that time yet. She felt upset that Hayley hadn't come to her, and she worried about how her daughter was coping. Later that day, when she was tucking her into bed, Gemma told Hayley that she'd found the bag, and gave her a hug. Hayley's little face crumpled as she said that she didn't know what to do and she was sorry, she was really sorry. Gemma reassured her that she'd done nothing wrong and she'd managed really well on her own, but now Gemma could help her and they would deal with it together.

Caitlin's dad offers his support

When Caitlin's first period started, her dad gave her a fleece-covered hot water bottle. It symbolises her dad's support and Caitlin uses it every month.

What if she starts bleeding away from home?

When I talk to prepubescent girls, one of the things they fear most about starting their periods is, 'What if I'm not at home?' Girls are increasingly worried about having their period at school, as the culture seems to be toughening up. Many schools forbid pupils to go to the toilet during lessons and penalise children who take too long moving classroom between lessons. Often girls are not aware of any school policy for girls who need to change their sanitary wear during or between lessons, how to communicate this need to a male teacher, or where they can ask for a pad if caught short. This is creating a lot of unnecessary anxiety, which we women must sort out. Contact your daughter's school and ask for clarity and assurance for our girls.

Many girls imagine that the blood will come gushing out, so give your daughter a realistic sense of what actually happens. Give her DIY emergency tips on how to catch the blood with a rolled-up wad of toilet paper so that she knows she can cope even if she has nobody to turn to and no pads with her. Give her a starter kit to carry in her bag with a pad, spare knickers, arnica and your mobile number, all safely zipped into a pencil case. No matter how well you have prepared your daughter, the start of her bleeding will come as a shock. Until now the sight of blood has indicated injury and pain, so explain that it's quite normal to feel weepy, overwhelmed and scared as well as excited. Explore how she imagines she will handle different scenarios: if she is at school, at a friend's, with her dad, or in town. Make sure she understands that having a period means that she can get pregnant if she has sex. Allow her to take it easy around the time of her monthly bleed.

. . . .

The first bleed is special – do what you can to take the anxiety out of the anticipation of it.

. . . .

Katy's first bleed happens at school

Katy noticed a brown stain in her pants when changing after gym at school. She felt embarrassed because she thought it was poo – her tummy wasn't feeling right, so she went to the sick room. The school nurse told her it might be her first period starting. She felt a bit panicky – even though her mum had told her all about it – and she just wanted to go home. She was worried that her mum would be cross at being called, but she wasn't. At home she helped Katy to put a pad in her pants, made hot chocolate, and they snuggled on the sofa watching their favourite film.

Early starters . . .

Imagine a girl playing. She is completely absorbed in an imaginary world that involves her teddy, a Lego house she has built and some loose change. Suddenly she looks up, a puzzled expression on her face. She jumps up and runs to the toilet.

This little girl is nine. She has just started her periods. She's lucky: her mother found her crying in the bathroom and explained to her what was happening. But she hated the blood and she didn't want to have to deal with it. She didn't want anyone else to know and she was worried about going to school. She felt like something terrible was happening and she just wanted it all to go away. Her mother was shocked too.

What might that little girl need? Hold her, let her be little. Listen to her, whatever she wants to say, without contradicting, reassuring or minimising. Let her be angry, sad, fearful, and let her know that her feelings are normal. Explain to her very simply what is happening, for now focusing on the physical changes instead of on her 'becoming a woman'. Reassure her that the bleeding will stop by itself and will happen again in a month or so. Tell her that it happens to all girls sometime between eight and eighteen years old and recount the story of when you started. Teach her how to keep clean, showing her how to use a sanitary pad and telling her when she will need to change it. Be willing to deal with it all for her until she is ready. She might like to chart her monthly cycle on a calendar and you can help her to notice if her eating habits or mood change with her cycle. Tell her teacher, asking for discretion, and find other girls who have started young. Give her a pencil case to hold pads and spare pants to take in her bag and reassure her that no one can tell when she is bleeding. For the first few months, let her stay home from school on her heaviest days until she gets used to managing her flow. Have fun. Take as much of the stress away as you can and do nice things: sofa snuggles, reading to her while she soaks in an Epsom salt bath, foot massage, Mother–Daughter Date. Give her a private gift to mark the special change in her body.

Susie's auntie helped with her being an early developer

Susie was only eight when her body started changing. By age ten she looked more like a teenager than the little girl she still was. Adults often mistook her for someone older and expected more of her. Susie was moody and confused. She still liked little girl games but she felt different from her friends. The boys teased her at school. Normally a happy, outgoing little girl, she started to withdraw. She hunched her shoulders to try and hide her womanly shape. Susie's mum hadn't felt ready for her little girl to go into puberty either and pretended it wasn't happening. It was Susie's auntie who came to the rescue. She insisted on treating Susie and her mother to a fancy bra-fitting. They went to a little lingerie boutique in town and all three had enormous fun trying on bras. They finished up at a cake shop, where they planned their next outing.

I HATE MY PERIODS!

For some time now I've been hearing of girls who are struggling at menarche. Girls who are incapacitated by cramping, flooding, inconsolable teariness, fiery furies or depression. Girls who are missing days of school every month, not just for their first few periods while they adjust to them. This is partly due to a number of factors that disrupt female hormones:

- Tap water contains synthetic hormones from the pill, as they are hard to filter out.
- Animal products (meat, milk, eggs) that are not organic may contain growth hormones and other chemicals to make livestock produce more milk and speed up reproduction.
- Hormone disruptors that mimic oestrogen leach from plastic water bottles and food packaging.
- Chemicals contained in oral contraceptive pills, morning-after pills, chemical abortions, contraceptive injections and implants are not only incredibly difficult for the body to get rid of, but are passed from mother to child in the womb.
- All these are exacerbated by increased stress (exams, family breakdown, radiation from mobiles, etc.).

Teens have been helped in various ways:

- Seeking help from professionals such as nutritionists, acupuncturists, homeopaths or herbalists.
- Not taking the pill (which only offers short-term relief and stores up problems for the future).
- Eating organic meat and dairy.
- Checking for vitamin and mineral deficiencies.
- Adding essential fatty acids (omega 3, 6, 9), probiotics and vitamin B complex to the diet.
- Cutting out endocrine disruptors such as trans-fats, artificial sweeteners and preservatives.

- Drinking filtered water from metal water bottles.
- Turning wifi and mobile phones off at night.
- Epsom salt baths – magnesium sulphate can be beneficial for menstrual cramps, is calming and soothing and promotes good sleep; for girls suffering from monthly discomfort, try one cup of BP grade Epsom salts in a bath three times a week before bedtime.

My heart goes out to all those girls whose early experience of monthly bleeding is debilitating or distressing. It will affect how they feel about becoming a woman. Problems at menarche indicate an imbalance, so take them seriously and find help.

. . . .

If we are going to have periods, let's have better ones!

. . . .

Menarche and menopause – menace or marvel?

Many older mothers are approaching menopause just as their daughters move into puberty. The daughter experiences hormonal changes as her body prepares to bleed monthly, whilst the mother experiences hormonal shifts as her body comes to the end of her monthly bleeding.

It is commonplace for both mother and daughter to suffer from cramping, flooding, spots, food cravings, moodiness and tiredness. Many mothers also struggle with hot flushes, insomnia, anxiety and a fierce longing for solitude. Women and girls often wonder, 'What is wrong with me?'

What if the answer is 'nothing'? Our bodies are working at keeping us well. At puberty and menopause, as well as in pregnancy, we are in a phase of great change and this makes us more sensitive. The messages that we receive from our bodies help us know that we need to take greater care of ourselves. We find that we must eat more carefully, get better rest, exercise, reduce stress and live in a more balanced way.

We may have been able to get away with doing too much, eating badly and staying up late but during puberty, pregnancy and menopause our symptoms summon us to boost our self-care in order to feel well. Expert guidance may be required to figure out what is needed. A girl in puberty may need to increase her intake of omega oils, learn tools for managing her emotions or benefit from extra rest. A woman in her forties may just need a magnesium supplement. Alternatively, she might need to find ways to relax more, or even reassess her whole life.

Many women who have gone through menopause enjoy being more able to put themselves first, and feel clearer about how they want to spend the next decades of their life. Our bodies can be the most amazing guides. While the messages may be inconvenient, insistent and persistent, when we listen and make the changes our body calls us to make, our sense of wellbeing increases. Perhaps the timing isn't wrong either. Those mothers who are experiencing the sensitivity of menopause will be reminded to teach their daughter to listen to what her own body needs during puberty.

TALKING ABOUT BLOOD

Gather some of your daughter's friends and their mothers so you can all talk about your bleeding time. You may need a pretext to get the conversation started such as watching a female comedian who jokes about periods. You will have women supporting girls – sharing their experiences of their first bleed and how their monthly cycle is now; women supporting women – offering sympathy and advice for difficult times, with howls of laughter for experiences shared; and girls supporting girls – daring to ask questions and making touching offers of support to one another.

The preteens in Girls Journeying Together are surprised by how much they enjoy the intimacy of hearing from older girls and women. Amidst laughter and a few tears we all learn a lot from each other. Girls hear things that their own mothers might not have thought to tell them: gems for managing mood swings, food cravings and cramps. Too many women have stories of menstrual suffering before they happened upon a solution. Let's encourage our girls to seek help sooner by talking freely about something so fundamental to our wellbeing.

Girl Talk – A girl's guide to periods

Our monthly cycle

A monthly cycle can be deeply reassuring. Each time my period comes I have a sense that all is well in my body – and it bothers me if ever it falters due to ill health, travel or stress. Even though menstruating might sometimes be inconvenient, uncomfortable or emotionally unsettling, I miss it when it fails to come. Nature's cycles give us a rhythm to live by – the cycle of seasons, the cycles of the moon and women's cycles can all provide a reassuring sense of pattern.

First, where does it all happen?

Make a triangle with your index fingers and thumbs and place your index fingers at the point where your legs meet your body. Your uterus is in that triangle, about the size of your fist. Leading into the top of the uterus on either side are two Fallopian tubes connecting to the ovaries where the eggs are stored. The ovaries are about the size of almonds and the eggs are mere pinpricks.

. . . .

Baby girls are born with all their eggs, all one million of them, so you started life inside your grandmother!

. . . .

Now the hormones

At puberty your hormones shift and that triggers lots of changes in your body. About a year after you first notice creamy marks in your underwear, you may find that your periods start. The hormones oestrogen and progesterone play a big part.

After your first few periods, your body settles into a rhythm. It begins each time with around twenty eggs ripening in one ovary while the lining in your uterus thickens, making it a healthy place for the egg to grow if it gets fertilised. Then the ovary releases the ripest egg, the rest are absorbed, and the egg begins its journey down the Fallopian tube to the uterus. This whole part of the process is called ovulation and takes eleven to twenty-one days.

. . . .

In our lifetime we'll release between four hundred and five hundred eggs; all the others are absorbed into the body.

. . . .

The egg spends two to three days travelling down the Fallopian tube to the uterus and, if fertilised, it embeds into the lining of the uterus and begins to grow. Your fertile period is two to three days before the egg is released and two to three days afterwards; during this week you can become pregnant if you have sex. If the egg is not fertilised it is absorbed into the uterus lining and after about two weeks the lining breaks away and comes out of the uterus through the cervix and through the opening in the vagina – and that's your period.

Your monthly cycle goes from the first day of one period to the first day of your next period and is usually between twenty-five and thirty-five days long. Some women are really regular and for others the length of their cycle varies.

. . . .

We bleed only about two to three tablespoons of blood each month. The rest is lining shed from the uterus, which still only amounts to about a third of a cup (maximum one cup) trickling out over three to eight days.

. . . .

Some girls can't wait to start menstruating, while others are less keen. It's perfectly normal to feel nervous and to have worries. Every girl needs an older woman who can answer her questions and concerns. There are some great internet sites and books written to help too.

. . . .

The average age for starting to menstruate is thirteen years, but it can be as early as eight and as late as eighteen and still be normal.

. . . .

A girl's first blood is a very important event, as it heralds her ability to conceive and bear a child – a key step along her journey towards womanhood. See if you can find a way to celebrate this.

Wings or no wings? A guide to menstrual products

When you're bleeding, you have choices for how to catch the blood.

Easy: disposable pads – thin pads of absorbent material that you stick inside the gusset of your underwear

- Some have wings to hold them in place, while others have a sticky strip.
- Different sizes depending on your size and lightness of flow.
- Better if they are organic, unbleached and unscented.

Better for the planet and the pocket: reusable pads – soft fabric pads that popper into your underwear

- Fabric pads are soft and pretty, but you do have to wash them.

Hidden away: tampons – a wad of cotton about the size of your little finger that goes inside you with a string attached to make it easy to pull out – instructions come with the tampons

- A tampon won't show when you're swimming, dancing or wearing tight clothes.
- Some have applicator tubes to help push the tampon in.
- Better if they are organic and unbleached.

- You can use these right from when you first start bleeding.
- They don't take away your virginity and can't get lost inside you.
- There is a rare risk of toxic shock syndrome, so change your tampon every four to six hours.

Other less common choices: moon cup, sponge, reusable cotton tampon

Caught without anything: wad of toilet paper

> *Sally's mum took her to the chemist long before she started her period and showed her where to find sanitary products, explained the different ones, and bought a small packet of pads to keep in the bathroom cabinet for when Sally would need them. Sally was a swimmer, though, and decided to try tampons so she wouldn't have to stop training. The first time, she couldn't get the tampon in and that put her off. Then she overheard the girls in her swimming team joking about how they found it helped to put one foot up on the toilet and she tried that – successfully.*

> *Louisa's mum was all about saving the planet – they recycled their rubbish, cycled to school and Louisa's mum had reusable sanitary pads. Louisa didn't like the idea of having to bring soiled pads home to wash them. But then her mother gave her a teen starter kit: beautiful soft pads, with a pouch to keep one in her bag. She ended up using reusable pads on days she was home and disposables when she was out.*

A text alert before your first period!

Wouldn't it be great if you got a text that gave you advance notice? 'Big news! Your first period will start next week on Wednesday at 5.30 p.m.'

You could make sure you'd be home, have pads organised and someone there with you.

Seeing blood in your knickers for the first time can be a shock. Until now blood has meant that there's something wrong, but your monthly bleed can become a reassuring regular sign that your body is working well. It also reminds us that we are special – girls and women who are menstruating can nurture life.

· ·

Your first period is an important event and a time to feel proud.

· ·

It's normal to have a whole mixture of feelings when it comes – frightened, excited, nervous, embarrassed, proud, grown-up, relieved, tearful, happy . . . If you don't feel like telling your parents straight away, find someone else to talk to. Women remember what it was like when they started and will want to support you. You are joining a very large club of all the girls and women around the world who bleed monthly. It's the most natural thing in the world, but it can take a bit of getting used to.

The first time, you may just find dark brown stains in your underwear; or the blood may flow more and be bright red. Don't worry: it will only ever be about a third of a cup, which trickles out over a few days. Although your period will end up coming monthly, at the beginning you might have one and then not have another one for a while, or it might come more often and take some time before it comes regularly.

As already described, you have a number of choices for how to catch the blood, and if you're caught out you can always wrap toilet paper several times around your hand to make an absorbent wad to put in your underwear.

Many girls and women find their monthly bleed to be a good thing, a cleansing, creative time of knowing more clearly how they feel. Some experience cramping or moodiness and need to find out about what to eat and how to take care of themselves to ease this.

You can't choose when your period will start. It will be sometime between eight and eighteen years old. Yours will come roughly two-and-a-half years after the first signs of puberty. So if you first noticed breast buds at the age of ten, then you're likely to be around twelve and a half when you have your first bleed. Whether you feel ready or not, it's good to make sure that you're a bit prepared.

Get some pads and carry one with some spare knickers in a little purse in your bag. Talk to older girls or women to find out what to expect, or read about it.

So even without a text alert you can still get yourself ready for your first period. Even if what you'd like to reply is, 'Actually, Sunday afternoon at 3 p.m. would be better', or, 'I'd like to postpone to next year'. Think about how you would like to celebrate your first period – it could be a special meal with your family, a little gathering of close friends, or a private treat by yourself in your bedroom. It is something to be proud of.

Teen PMS and cramping

Most girls and women find that having their period does not mean that ordinary life has to stop. They can still carry on with normal activities, including sports, swimming and dancing. However, slowing down a bit at this time can also be lovely, especially if your life is usually lived at a fast pace.

. . . .

Women who experience premenstrual tension or cramping are getting stronger messages from their bodies that they need to take special care at this time of the month.

. . . .

Premenstrual syndrome (PMS) or premenstrual tension (PMT) is the symptoms that some women experience just before they start bleeding each month. These can include pimples, breast tenderness, bloating, weight gain, headaches, tiredness, irritability, mood swings, heightened emotions and clumsiness. Many women don't experience any of these things, or only mildly, so don't assume that you are destined to become a swollen, angry, spotty thing every month.

Many women find that they feel things more acutely and see things more clearly around this time, and it benefits them to ease off a little and take some time alone. In some cultures, and in times gone by, women always slowed down around the time of their monthly bleed, and other women stepped in to share their load. Slowing down can also reduce uncomfortable premenstrual symptoms.

If you are bothered by PMS there are many things you can do to ease it:

Tired? Sleep and rest more. Avoid stimulants like tea, coffee, chocolate and sugar – they will lift you temporarily and then drop you down with a thump.

Irritable? Take time alone. Then you'll not have the worry of saying something you might regret later. It can be a good time to listen to music, read, write, draw, paint or create.

Breast tenderness? Take evening primrose oil and cut back on salt.

Pimples, bloating, overeating, headaches, mood swings? Take greater care over what you eat for a bit: more fruit and vegetables, plenty of water, good proteins (organic if possible), whole grains. Cut down on fried things, red meat, processed foods, white bread and fizzy drinks. Tedious, perhaps, but just see how much better you feel.

Cramping is not experienced by all women, or at every period, or that strongly for many. It's caused by the contractions that expel the lining of the uterus (so it's a sneak preview of how labour pains might feel, only much weaker). You may feel like reaching for the painkillers at the first tingles of pain, but there are many other things you can do to ease your discomfort naturally.

Cramping can be nature's way of saying, 'Slow down and take care of yourself.'

- Rather than pushing yourself to carry on, try snuggling on the sofa with a hot water bottle on your tummy, and a good book.
- Breathe gently down into your belly and imagine breathing the pain out with every outbreath.
- Take a warm bath, adding a large cup of Epsom salts and a few drops of lavender oil.
- Exercise, even if at first it feels like the last thing you fancy, as it can ease cramping by increasing the blood flow to your uterus. A walk, yoga or even tidying your room can help.
- Massage your ankles, feet and belly gently.
- If none of this works, seek help from a naturopath, homeopath, acupuncturist, herbalist or GP.

Heavy bleeding is not uncommon for teens. If your period lasts for longer than a week, or if you need to change your pad or tampon after less than an hour several times in a row, then your heavy bleeding (menorrhagia) needs to be addressed. It's usually due to a hormone imbalance, but it could indicate the presence of something like fibroids or endometriosis, so see a doctor to check it out. If the doctor suggests oral contraceptives, there are many natural alternatives that you may find to be just as effective and that are better for you. Find an expert naturopath, herbalist, homeopath or nutritionist.

Don't suffer in silence. It's quite normal for your first few periods to be quite intense, but if they haven't settled down after a few months then find help to make things better. Periods shouldn't bring suffering month after month.

Tanya and her mum both found relief from painful periods

After a year in a Girls Journeying Together group, Tanya felt quite excited about starting her periods. She was at school when her first period came, and although she felt fine she asked her mum to collect her. The rest of the day was special, just hanging out with Mum at home, making a couple of calls to tell Granny and a close auntie, and baking chocolate brownies. She didn't have another period for a few months, but her next one was really painful and Tanya felt very teary; suddenly it seemed daunting to have a lifetime of menstruation stretching ahead of her. The next one was worse still, and came after only three weeks. Tanya was dreading her next period. Her mother talked to other mothers whose daughters were having similar difficulties and they recommended going on the pill. Somehow this didn't seem like a healthy long-term solution, so she took her daughter to a naturopath, who suggested that Tanya cut back on fatty and processed foods, take a herbal supplement, and rest on the first day of her next period. Tanya tried this and it made a bit of a difference, but still she felt weepy and uncomfortable. She kept going with this advice, though, and over six months it all got a lot better. She still felt a bit weepy on the first day of her period, and it was a good idea to have a quieter day. She no longer feared her period coming and she knew what would make it easier, even if sometimes she didn't follow that advice and had a harder time of it!

To support her daughter, Tanya's mum also followed the naturopath's advice and had pain-free and manageable bleeding for the first time in her life. She wished that she had known about this years ago.

PART II

The chaos of adolescence

CHAPTER FOUR

Answering the big teen questions

The teen years are a time of exploration, blossoming and self-consciousness, while young people try to define who they are and decide what they want. It's tempting to make fun of our teenagers as they swerve all over the place in their thoughts, feelings and behaviour. But we need to remember that they are following their evolutionary need to explore their identity as they move from the dependence of childhood towards adult independence. One of the major problems facing teenagers today is that we are not giving them what they need to grow up.

In my work I have seen time and again that when someone cannot follow their true nature, the likelihood of developing mental health issues can significantly increase. Education, for example, can stifle children's inner need for self-guided exploration; we parents can put immense pressure on them and on ourselves to fit our idea of a successful upbringing while we lose sight of what really feeds our teenagers' intuition, dreams and sense of self-honouring.

I explore some of these issues at the beginning of this chapter and then move on to discuss how you can help your daughter build a robust sense of self by:

- Helping her to answer the big 'Who am I?' question.
- Supporting her to follow her dreams, trust her intuition and know about her roots.

- Learning how to let her go while staying connected.
- Enabling her gradually to become the boss of her life, her money, her space and her time.

BIG TEEN QUESTIONS

When you think back to your teen years, can you remember what you wanted to know about yourself? These are the things that your daughter will probably also want to learn:

- Do people like me? What do they like about me? Do they like me for me?
- Do I look okay?
- What do I really like doing? What am I good at? What am I going to do when I grow up?
- What do I believe in?
- Who am I?

Being a teen can be a chaotic business. Your daughter is going to question your authority, your family's values, her background, cultural traditions, the school establishment, her beliefs, your beliefs, just about everything! It's healthy – she is working out who she is separate from you but in the context of her upbringing. She will try out new behaviours, she will copy things from people she admires, she's experimenting. She will be more critical of you and your parenting. She is going to appear more selfish – she's got a lot of figuring out to do and this takes self-focus. She is to be admired: it takes courage to try new ways, risking ridicule.

A parent's job is to be there, not centre stage but in the wings. Your daughter needs to feel your supportive gaze, not a judgemental glare. She is going to mess up, she is going to say things that she regrets, wear things she will later be horrified by, do things that aren't really her. Her experimentation is harder to watch when she is trying to fit in by doing what her friends are doing. Or worse if you feel she is being led astray by the crowd she is with. Young people will do stuff in a group that they'd never do on their own. It can seem like your daughter loses her sense of what is safe and right. But tread carefully: these friends are an essential part of her tribe and she needs them as she journeys towards adulthood. Growing up isn't easy and her ability to find the support of friends along the way is essential. You will alienate her if you constantly criticise them or her.

Encourage her self-expression and exploration, allow her to make mistakes and help her to learn from them by being attentive; not judging, but waiting for her to reflect on what didn't work. That doesn't mean you let her do just anything. You will need to hold firm boundaries – that's your job too. Some things you may ban until she is a certain age, some things will never be acceptable. However, it's important for her maturation that you begin to hand some of life's decisions over to her. She will fight you less if she senses that you will only step in when absolutely necessary. Of course you want to guide her away from the worst excesses or any real danger, but too often we adults think we can spare our young from making the same mistakes we made merely by instructing them.

Besides, teens are experts. They don't need our advice – they know it all already! They have the 'arrogance of youth' giving them the courage to go forward by being adamant they know the way. Resist the urge to cut your daughter down. Allow her that show of strength; it doesn't need to threaten you. She needs you quietly sure of yourself because it makes her feel safer.

These are precious years. She is changing and growing and you are a vital part of that. You can't do her growing up for her and you can't control the direction she is going to take in life, but you do have an important role in equipping her for what lies ahead. You can be a sounding-board for her questioning. When her self-analysis spirals off into anxiety and over-thinking, you can bring her back to earth. Most importantly, you can keep loving her as she solidifies her sense of who she is. It's exciting and scary – for you and for her. She is going to irritate you, terrify you, sadden you and entertain you.

IS OUR CULTURE HELPING OR HINDERING OUR TEENAGERS?

Some aspects of our educational system, combined with the expectations that parents hold for their children and for themselves, put unnecessary and increasing pressure on teenagers at a vulnerable time in their development.

Education

How many adults are bored, uninspired, unmotivated or without direction? A fair few. How many young children are? Not many. So what happens in between?

Children learn by playing. They experiment, observe and test. By the time they are teenagers they have been taught to sit still, and listen, and be tested, and that playing is just for kids. If they are finding it hard to motivate themselves at school, they are not necessarily being rebellious, but they do need our help.

Teenagers have an imperative to question, explore and find out for themselves. If this is discouraged they can lose motivation. It's not actually a good time to insist that they study and be tested. Happily, some teachers have found ingenious ways of working with their teenage pupils, creating the space for them to explore their own ideas and arrive at their own conclusions before introducing them to the ideas of others.

We learn by making connections – sparked by an interest – and then exploring and expanding our understanding. The national curriculum, delivered by teachers to large groups of pupils who will later be tested on what they can remember, aims to do this but it just can't cater to the diverse and individual needs of each child. Inevitably our children's curiosity is stifled and directed. Pupils' understanding of the world is parcelled up into disconnected subjects that they often only learn because they know that they will be examined on them. Children stop following their hearts and learn to follow someone else's plan. The plan may be well intentioned and could even serve them well, but not if it means they find that there's no time (or approval) to do what they love as well. Children are told that they must do well in school so that they will get a good job. Sadly, however, adults often do not enjoy their 'good jobs', and children notice this.

Susie's parents were able to help her to find her own way

Susie was being prised from her mother's arms, where she was clinging for dear life. Five weeks into secondary school it was getting harder for her to be there instead of easier. She was doing okay with the work, but there were just too many children, classroom changes and different teachers. The school had been great, assigning someone to help her, but school had never been an easy place for Susie and it was getting worse. At home Susie was funny, bookish and passionate about styling hair. But come Monday morning she was a changed child and it was heartbreaking for her parents to watch. The day Susie was pulled from her mother's arms by a well-meaning teacher something snapped inside her mum. This felt so wrong. It wasn't the school's fault, but it was damaging her little girl. She took her out. Just for a little while, to give Susie a chance to feel better about herself. To have a break from the tears and sulks. And Susie finally felt like she'd been heard. At first she slept, a lot. And read. Her mum found her a maths and English course online and arranged for her to sweep up at the local hair salon. Over the next few months her old Susie came back. A Susie who bounced in from an afternoon at the salon full of stories and ideas for hair-dos. A Susie who no longer thought that there was something wrong with her for not thriving at school. A Susie who, a few years later, took herself to the local adult education centre to learn coding so that she could design a phone app for people to try out different hairstyles before committing.

. . . .

If our children learn how to learn and acquire a love of learning,
then they are well equipped. Enabling this is true education.

. . . .

How would life be different in your home if your child's internal wisdom could be trusted?

What if we were to encourage our children to play more, and as teenagers to explore their own ideas more – to make mistakes, to take a hobby really seriously, to learn for themselves? All too often children's fascinations are swept aside in favour of more valued activities or areas of learning. Or their lives are so scheduled that there's no time for creative play. Yet so many eminent adults cite their success as seeded by a childhood passion started in their bedroom or the shed. To sit in a classroom and be told what to know and how to think can be soul-destroying for many. Childhood is not the time to fill our children's heads with information. In this Wikipedia-age, that part is easy. Notice how they will naturally inform themselves of whatever they need to know when it is something they are fascinated by. What is more elusive, and more precious to find, is what makes their hearts sing. If you need to teach your child anything, teach her to pay attention to her intuition and then teach her how to be resourceful – to sift through facts, feel confident about her ability to learn new things, develop her own opinions and listen to what feels right. This will serve her well in adult life when she is tackling any new task.

. . . .

Let our children's heads be full of their own ideas, plans and
projects – and their days full of the realisation of some of them.

. . . .

Success stories of school failures

Aretha Franklin, a child prodigy, left school at fifteen and went on to win eighteen Grammys. Lady Gaga and Madonna dropped out of formal education. Mary-Kate Olsen and Muriel Siebert both cut their education short and went on to become entrepreneurs worth billions. Houdini's first escape is said to have been from school at twelve and he went on to become a great escapologist. Elton John and Richard Branson both left their studies to go on to do what they loved.

Too much pressure on our teenagers?

What is your vision for your daughter? Most parents start by saying that they just want their children to be happy. Healthy and happy. We might go on to say that we want our child to find fulfilling work, love and be loved, be self-assured, *and* be happy. But she might be happy just eating chips and skipping school. What then? We have to admit that we have our own ideas about where her true happiness lies.

Children are struggling under the pressure to realise the goals that are set for them. As they strive to meet what is expected of them, they lose touch with what they actually wish for themselves.

What parents say they want for their child is very different from what teens think their parents want from them: do well in school, then get a good job. Succeed in chosen hobbies. Eat sensibly. Go to bed on time. Have friends who are a good influence. Do as you are told: help out, clear up, be nice. Act responsibly, don't be confrontational, be sunny and sweet. Stay clear of drugs. Wait for sex. Oh, and be happy.

It is easier for us to focus on exam results and messy bedrooms and slip into 'Have you done ... ?' and 'Shouldn't you ... ?' rather than concentrating on how to boost our teens' confidence and nurture the acorns of their dreams.

. . . .

Get behind your child's passions or get out of the way so she can pursue them.

. . . .

Even if your daughter's fascinations seem fickle, when you prioritise them you are showing her how important it is for her to follow her own interests. Trust that within her is the impulse to seek out what makes her heart sing and to discover where her talents lie. This is easier if you understand and approve of your child's dreams, but if you truly want a happy child you will support her in whatever it is that she loves.

She may want to:

- Plant flowers to save the bees rather than study stigma and stamens.
- Draw and dance rather than solve simultaneous equations.
- Perfect her recipe for slime.
- Make videos to post online.
- Play her guitar and make up songs.
- Free range in your kitchen to make chocolate cake and chicken curry.
- Earn money and spend Saturday in town spending that money.

. . . .

A child who has been allowed to develop her true self is more likely to be a happy self – right through into adulthood.

. . . .

Too much pressure on parents?

We parents put pressure on ourselves to get it right, as if there were some sort of 'right' that we could 'get'. Culturally there are great expectations on parents to provide more for our children. More quality time, more after-school activities, more tutoring, more toys, more nourishing food, more, more, more. Many parents drive themselves hard (and their children too) out of fear that their children might miss out or fall behind.

It is paradoxical when this drive to provide the best for our children necessitates that parents work many hours away from their children to be able to afford this 'best'. Often our children are in the hands of others for huge chunks of their waking hours, and we expect those carers and teachers to nurture, nourish and socialise them.

Culturally we have slipped into a belief that in order to become decent adults our children should be moulded and adapted, tended and taught.

We behave towards them as if they are a work in progress – *our* work in progress. By taking over responsibility for who they are, we take away the possibility of them being responsible for themselves. We risk raising children who do not trust their intuition, do not know their own minds or how to make their own healthy and wise choices. This is damaging to children and places them at risk. The world is full of adults who don't know how to listen to themselves.

I'm not advocating a parenting style that lacks loving involvement. And I don't think children like overly permissive parenting, or to be burdened by too much choice or too much responsibility for their overall wellbeing. I believe children do well when we have high expectations of honest, age-appropriate and responsible behaviour, especially when we are able to model this through our example rather than merely prescribing it.

WHO AM I?

Your daughter discovers her answers to the biggest question of them all, 'Who am I?', by listening to her inner voice, following her dreams and having an awareness of her ancestry. As a person finds peace with who she is, and lives according to her core beliefs, she frees herself from needing to fit in.

Daring to dream

Children are inspiring: they watch someone and immediately imagine that they too could be a superhero, pop star or Olympic athlete. Children are brilliant at reaching for the stars. They imagine an adult life of great possibility: running a riding stables or flying jets, writing a best-seller or designing clothing for celebrities. Adults do these things, and children are inspired.

We adults must refrain from pouring our cold reality onto their dreams, believing we are protecting them from unrealistic hopes, sparing them from disappointment. Is it really better not to dream the impossible than to try to see how far you can get? If six-year-old Joanne Rowling hadn't believed herself capable of being a writer, writing her first story, 'Rabbit', we wouldn't have Hogwarts and Harry Potter. If that small Jamaican boy Usain hadn't dared to dream of being the fastest runner in the whole wide world, we wouldn't have had the Olympic legend that was Bolt.

Children see an injustice and declare that they will stop it. They have the audacity to hope for the best from people and sometimes this brings out the best in people. Take fourteen-year-old Julia Bluhm, who was concerned about how many girls in her ballet class considered themselves to be fat and dared to ask *Seventeen* magazine to stop photoshopping its photos. After 84,000 people signed her petition the magazine made a commitment not to alter the body size or face shape of the girls and models and to feature a diverse range in its pages. Or take nine-year-old Martha Payne, who commented daily on her school dinners, raising the standard of school meals and more than £10,000 for a charity providing meals for UK school children.

Every person who has achieved great things has a tale of modest beginnings and those who first inspired them. Children dare to dream big. The sky is the limit when you are six or even sixteen.

Parents' encouragement is vital. Your child needs you to believe in her – a parent's opinion is such an influential thing for a child. Take her interests seriously and help her to follow her passions. A person does well in life when she is doing something that she cares about and enjoys. In a world full of people doing jobs they don't particularly like, and surrounded by adults dousing children's grand plans in realism before they can even try them out, our children need us to support them in following their hearts.

If you weren't able to follow your dreams as a teen, you will need extra courage to be there for your teenager as she follows hers. All too easily she can hold herself back through lack of self-belief, finances, opportunity or willingness to expend effort. Challenges can strengthen us and, if those around her believe something is possible, it helps her to believe it too. We all have our 'disabilities' – some more obvious and some more debilitating. The Paralympics gives us the chance to see that the most crippling disadvantages can be overcome.

Do you know what your child dares to dream?

· ·

Dreams are delicate. Go carefully – they are all too easily crushed.

· ·

Children thank me for not helping

Miss Sophie, our local dance teacher, produces a show for all her dancers to perform in the local theatre. Afterwards, my daughter, who was in her show, and my son, who watched it, were inspired to create their own dance show. And they did, in three days, with ten friends, and performed it to over seventy people in our village hall!

Twelve children gathered at our home one Monday morning during half-term, full of hope and overflowing with ideas, and by Wednesday evening they were ready to perform a half-hour show. They chose the story, the music and the costumes; they choreographed dances, set up lighting, made tickets, designed programmes and had an absolute ball. Imagine twelve enthusiastic children in one room, with a deadline two days away. Now understand that of these twelve children there were five sets of siblings, ranging in age from six to eleven, each with their flash points. Think about how they would have to organise themselves, with all their different expectations and concentration spans. And remember that they had no adult instruction. All I did was offer them our home, send emails, authorise payment for music downloads, book the hall and provide copious snacks. Originally they had thought that three mornings would be enough, but after the first morning they all decided to spend six and a half hours together for the subsequent

*two days, before going home and working some more. My house
was abuzz with activity. Great future entrepreneurs!*

*The children who took part had a dream and they made it
come true.*

*The parents watching were impressed by what their children
were capable of.*

*The children in the audience were inspired to make their
dreams happen too.*

*The children gave me a card after the show thanking me 'for
NOT helping'!*

School years can sometimes take their toll when it comes to children
learning to follow their dreams. So much of teens' time is spent at school,
studying for exams in only twenty possible subjects. Many feel this
isn't bringing them any closer to the work they wish to do or the people
who can help them learn what they will need to know, and they become
disheartened.

. . . .

Our children need courage to hold fast to their dreams.

. . . .

You can help your daughter to follow her dreams by paying attention to
what brings her joy and finding ways for her to follow that passion:

- Help her to spend time with adults she admires and whose advice
  she respects.
- Really listen to her as she talks enthusiastically about something.
- Read the book she is raving about or ask her to show you what she
  likes to watch.
- Ask her to teach you how to use her favourite social media tool.
- Help her pursue the activities she loves.
- Put her in contact with adults who are working in areas that
  fascinate her.

- Help her to self-publish.
- Let go of your dreams for her, making space for her dreams for herself.

And don't get attached to her dreams, as they may change as she grows.

Demi needed a reason to study

Demi enjoyed seeing her friends at school, but as the pressure to be studious intensified she became increasingly bored. At home she'd sooner spend time with her hamsters than do her homework. Her dad downloaded some nature programmes for her to watch and her mum arranged for her to spend a day helping out at a nearby animal rescue centre. Demi ended up volunteering there every weekend, and by talking to staff she discovered that with the right qualifications she could train to become an animal care worker. Suddenly she found motivation for studying biology, maths and English so that she would be eligible to apply for an apprenticeship a few years down the line.

Does your daughter know her own mind?

Does your daughter know what intuition feels like? Is she allowed to trust and follow this?

Having a daughter who knows her own mind can be challenging, but if you celebrate it she is more likely to find a path in life that really suits *her*.

Having a child who is full of ideas, passions and ideals can be exhausting, but if you encourage it she is more likely to think things through for herself and make good choices.

Having a daughter who is sensitive can be inconvenient at times, but if you honour her sensitivity she will feel able to pay attention to that funny feeling that tells her a situation isn't safe and get herself away from it.

Much in our culture dissuades us from listening to our gut feelings. Young children rarely have as much time with their parents as they would choose, are made to eat foods they don't fancy, and have to stick with teachers they don't warm to and spend time with children who are mean or who they clash with. Children are swamped by advertising that encourages them not to like the way they look, the possessions that they have or the life they are leading.

. . . .

Our children are taught not to pay attention to what they really want or how they really feel.

. . . .

You can help your daughter to be the girl who:

- Knows her own mind and does what she enjoys.
- Finds the words to stand up to someone who is a bully.
- Chooses not to shoplift because it feels wrong, even when her friends are urging her to.
- Pulls herself and her friend out of the party when things are getting a bit out of hand.
- Says no to drugs.
- Avoids the boy who makes her feel uneasy.
- Walks away from the man who is acting strangely at the bus stop.

Our children will only know to trust their intuition and act on their gut feelings if they've already had a lifetime of having their feelings listened to and taken seriously:

- Talk to her about recognising the quiet voice of reason and paying attention to it.
- Notice when she expresses an interest and help her to develop that.
- Support her passions and help her to shrink the disliked bits of her life.

- Teach her to notice how her body feels when something isn't quite right – girls usually find that their tummy, shoulders, mouth or hands alert them.
- Discuss strategies for how to respond when she doesn't feel at ease – text you, find a friend, take five minutes in the toilet to think clearly, seek a trusted adult, leave.

Sometimes we say we want strong, independent, confident daughters, but then we suppress those qualities when they thwart our own purpose. If you want your daughter to honour herself, *you* must honour her.

. . . .

Listen. Respect. Respond.

. . . .

Sammy listens to her gut instincts

Breathless, Sammy burst through the door. She seemed excited. 'There's a man on the bus and I sort of know him 'cos he often talks to me and he's nice and everything, but today he didn't get off at his normal stop – he stayed on and got off at my stop and I felt funny, you know in my tummy, like when there's a scary bit in a film, and so I ran all the way home. I don't think he followed me.' Her mother stopped what she was doing and got Sammy to explain again. She told Sammy she'd done well to listen to her gut. Then they talked about what she'd do tomorrow if the man was on the bus again, and talked to her or got off at her stop.

It's quite possible that there was nothing sinister to worry about – but Sammy had been encouraged to pay attention to her instincts and act on them without turning it into a drama, and this will stand her in good stead.

Abigail doesn't know her own mind

Janice kept a tidy house. She liked things a certain way. Kids polite and well dressed, home-cooked meals, homework completed, set bedtimes. She'd had depression when the kids were younger but she was much better now, as long as she kept on top of things. Her daughter Abigail had learnt to do what she was asked, to keep from stressing her mum. Abigail's best friend Tracey liked to get her own way and Abigail just found it easier to let her. So when Tracey started drinking, Abigail followed. And when Tracey wanted to skip an afternoon of school, Abigail did too. Once when she stayed the night, Tracey wanted to fool around, and even though Abigail wasn't sure if she fancied it really, she let it happen. When it came to making her subject choices at school Abigail had no idea what she liked to study, so she copied Tracey. Abigail was so used to pleasing others that she had no idea how to please herself or make her own decisions.

Letting boredom bite

What if your daughter doesn't seem to have any particular passions or special interests?

Embrace boredom! Plan for a whole chunk of unorganised time so your child can ask herself, 'How can I amuse myself today?' No outings, extra sports training, summer schools or camps. We become so accustomed to the routines of busy activity that we no longer know what we might like to do when nothing's been scheduled.

When lives are busy, children tend to resort to slumping in front of a screen as soon as they have a break. You may need to negotiate a wifi-free patch of time in order to extricate your teen from the digital world long enough to let that wellspring of creativity be activated. Then maybe she can remember how to design her own life: to float through the day, attracted to particular pastimes, foods, friends. To allow boredom to surface, and stay feeling it long enough to see what happens next ...

Discovering the benefits of boredom

Bethany fell ill right at the start of her daughters' summer holidays. At first she tried to summon up the energy to arrange outings and playdates to make the most of the holidays, but that made her health worse. Both children were forced to entertain themselves, which initially they did with screens; however, one ended up sewing herself a pair of shorts by following a YouTube video, the other one taught herself 'Greensleeves' on the keyboard, and the two girls had a laugh in the kitchen preparing all their own meals.

Her ancestors give her roots

In New Zealand the Maori people traditionally introduce themselves by first giving the name of their nearest mountain and river, then their tribe, their sub-tribe, their *marae* (sacred meeting place), and finally their name. Their greeting, or *mihimihi*, gives recognition to place and heritage forming a major part of who a person is.

In our European culture we too recognise that family and class play an important part in who someone is. We tend to use a person's occupation as a key indicator, as well as how they look, sound and behave. First impressions are powerful, and we infer a lot about a person from these first clues. Teenagers' experimentation with their appearance, speech and behaviour is a crucial part of their exploration into who they are. You can help to ground this experimentation by giving your daughter knowledge of her ancestry. Who are her people and where did they come from? This gives her roots, and having roots will give her a strong foundation from which to flourish and blossom.

Even if her ancestry doesn't seem that important, or you have moved away from your family of origin, share stories with her about her relations. It may help her to make sense of who she is.

Catrina's aunt gives her a sense of pride

Catrina hated how she looked. When she looked at photos of herself all she could see was an enormous nose. Friends teased her about it. As soon as she could, as soon as she left home and could afford to, she was going to have it made smaller. Her mum wouldn't approve, but her mum didn't have to live with a nose like hers. One day she confided in her auntie and to her amazement her auntie just started laughing. Scrabbling about in her desk drawer, her auntie explained that her great-grandmother had felt exactly the same way but in those days there wasn't plastic surgery. She produced a photo, 'There, look – look at that nose. If you think yours is big, look at hers!' Catrina had to agree that that was one big nose. Her curiosity was piqued: that man in the photo with the little cap on, was that her great-grandfather, and was he Jewish? 'Yes, sure, didn't you know?' 'No. Were they in the war?' 'That's what brought us over here. They were refugees, but no one talks about it much because of everything that happened.' 'What happened?' Catrina listened to her auntie, enthralled to hear stories about her family. A few years later, her auntie overheard Catrina retorting, 'Lay off, that's my Jewish nose you're insulting.'

LETTING HER GO WHILE STAYING CONNECTED

To enable our children to grow up fulfilling their potential, parents have a lifetime of letting go, from the moment of giving birth and cutting the umbilical cord. While this can be liberating for both parent and child, it can also be scary and painful. Staying connected while letting go is key. As parents we search for the right balance between ensuring safety and allowing freedom. Some parents cling on, others flip-flop between letting go and not, while others manage to gradually release their children as they grow.

We have to trust that our children will be capable. *Our children need us to believe in their competence.*

We have to trust that they will survive their mistakes. *Our children need the experience of learning from their mistakes.*

We have to trust ourselves to know when to loosen our hold and when to rein them in. *Our children's behaviour will guide us.*

Clinging on – when a parent is very risk-averse and constantly steps in to protect her child, it becomes hard for that child to be able to assess danger for herself. Research has shown that paradoxically these children can be at greater risk of harm in the long term, as they are less experienced at making decisions and taking responsibility for themselves.[1]

Flip-flopping – some parents find that by turning a blind eye to what is going on they can avoid the stress of constantly needing to make new age-appropriate boundaries with a child who is rightly pushing at those boundaries. It's confusing to a child when parents oscillate between saying no to everything and saying yes to everything.

Releasing gradually – sometimes parents are able to achieve that delicate dance of standing back, releasing their offspring to make their own way while at the same time counselling against danger.

Sometimes the hardest work of parenting is to get our 'selves' out of the way. Adults who were over-cosseted as children will often have a tendency either to repeat this with their own children or to react against it and be too liberal. If as a child you were bullied, or as a teen you went

1   Susan Davis & Nancy Eppler-Wolff, *Raising Children Who Soar: A Parent's Guide to Healthy Risk-taking in an Uncertain World* (Teachers College Press, 2009).

off the rails, it's hard not to fear that your own child will go the same way. But our children need us to see them as they are rather than through the spectacles of who we were. Try not to parent your child how you would have liked your parents to have been with you – but instead parent your child in the way *she* needs to be parented. When you consider the character of your child, you can assess how much holding and how much encouraging and how much freedom would best serve her development towards becoming a self-assured, competent and free-flying adult.

Letting go is integral to parenting, but it's not without its griefs and is best done in the company of others.

Alice tended to cling on to her kids

Alice grew up in the countryside and now she was raising her girls in the city. She lay in bed awake thinking of all the urban dangers. When they were young the girls had been happy to stay close to their mother, but now they were pushing to do things she just couldn't allow. They couldn't walk to the park on their own, they couldn't play with someone until Alice had met their parents, they couldn't take public transport, they couldn't go swimming without her ... To the girls the list seemed endless. By the time they were in their late teens the two girls had responded in opposite ways. Natalie had rebelled: she ignored curfews, hung out with a disapproved-of crowd, and did whatever she liked, barely speaking to her mother. Louise had gone all mousey, scared to speak out, fearful of anything new and reluctant to leave her mother's side.

Cathy had flip-flop parenting

Cathy wanted to stay out later than she was normally allowed to, but her parents wouldn't let her. A rule is a rule and they were sticking to it. She tried explaining that this was a one-off request because the film they wanted to watch didn't finish until after her curfew. She tried pleading and promising extra good behaviour. She begged: all the other girls were going, it was a birthday outing, she didn't want to be left out. She tried threatening to go anyway. She tried asking in the morning, after school, at bedtime. Eventually she wore them down; her mother snapped, 'Right, go! Do what you want. I don't care. Come in as late as you please. You will anyway.' Although Cathy seemed to have got what she wanted, she hadn't really. She wanted to be able to negotiate and compromise with her parents, instead she got what she often got: flip-flop parenting – rigid rules followed by abandonment of any restrictions. She never got the chance to think through why her parents wanted her home early, or whether this was a good time to make an exception, or how late is too late, because it just became a fight for getting her own way.

Staying safe through risk-taking

I was not a mother who rounded every corner in the house (with special plastic curves for sharp edges) trying to make her toddler's world safe. The world is not safe, but it's not that dangerous either if children learn what to look out for. I allowed my children to tumble off a piece of furniture that was wobbly rather than reaching out to steady it. My reasoning: this time I am here, keeping an eye, here to catch if a bad fall looks likely; next time I might not be. I wanted my children to learn to assess their own safety. The world is not curved, soft and stable, and children are safer for knowing to test for stability before climbing, knowing that zips can pinch and to carry glass carefully. A childhood is better when not peppered with constant anxiety-inducing cries of, 'Be careful!' 'Don't run!' 'You'll burn yourself!' 'You'll fall!' I hoped that by slipping and getting a little bit bruised my children would learn how to take good care of themselves and trust their instinct for self-preservation.

Our toddlers grow up into teens and we have a new set of risks to worry about. Instead of sharp corners and hot pans, it's late nights and unfinished homework, sex and cigarettes. Just as it is for toddlers, our teens are made safer by learning from their own experiences. It can be hard for us to trust our children to make enough of the right decisions to be safe, and tempting to tell them what to do. Telling people what to do rarely works.

I'm not saying leave your teen to it. Quite the opposite. Our teens need the same quality of attention that toddlers do. And just as I would alert a toddler to the possibility of something being unsafe – 'That looks wobbly', or 'Thinner branches aren't as strong as those thick ones' – so too I would inform my teenagers of the dangers in their environment.

By involving yourself in your teen's world, you can earn a privileged place as trusted guide by not freaking out when she makes a mistake, and listening while she figures out where she went wrong. Inform yourself about all the things that worry you. Find out about what keeps young people away from drugs, how to talk about drinking, tackle bullying, the after-effects of the morning-after pill and how to deal with self-harming. Then you will know how to discuss these issues when they crop up in the news, in a film or in your neighbourhood. Don't assume that everything will be covered in school. Make it okay to talk about these common teen concerns in your home so that your daughter is well informed and knows that you are open to discussing tough issues.

Parenting a teen is a diplomatic art. Stay present. Know when to be in the background. Observe with vigilance. Offer vital information. Step back and allow her to experiment and discover for herself. Only interfere if absolutely necessary.

Jemma learned the hard way how to stay safe

Jemma's parents were strict. No telly until her homework was done. Skirts not too short, hair not too crazy, modest make-

up, no lipstick. No going into town on her own, no staying out past ten, no sleepovers in term time, no parties unless the family was known. No boyfriends who didn't share the family's religion. So many rules to live by that when Jemma left home to go to university she went a bit wild. She had a lot of catch-up experimenting to do with how she dressed, who she made friends with and what they got up to together. She kept her parents at a distance because she knew they'd disapprove. For a year or so she made a lot of risky choices until she began to find her own sense of what was right for her.

Allowing her to learn for herself

Life would be so much easier if we were spared the 'Why?' or the 'Just a minute . . .' or the extended debate designed for a wriggle-out.

* * *

Compliant, agreeable children seem easy to parent, but do you really want a child who quietly acquiesces?

* * *

Children are designed to question – it's how they learn. Toddlers and teens especially are engaged in an intense period of self-exploration. How can they possibly figure out their own mind, their values, their sense of right, if we are constantly telling them what to do? Adults are great at having good reasons for telling our children how to be: 'She needs to learn.' 'It's for her own good.' 'I know what's best for her – I've been around, seen it, done it.' 'It's good manners.' We interfere in our children's dress sense, food, friends, homework, hobbies, education and downtime. We live in a culture that fundamentally mistrusts children to know how to grow up well. Society prescribes constant management of children by adults, and parents feel obliged to try to fulfil this expectation.

. . . .

It's an uncomfortable connection to make – if you tell her what to do, she will be more likely to let others do so too.

. . . .

When you don't tell your child what to do, I hope you will find that she then makes sound decisions for herself and turns to you for advice when she needs it. Handing the reins over to our children needs to be gradual and age appropriate. The role of the parent shifts from instructing to informing, and then only when asked. Habits of micromanaging are hard to break. So next time your teen leaves the house without a coat, you could bite your tongue. Let her get wet, feel cold, and then she will remember what is needed to stay warm and dry next time. If we don't give our children responsibility for minor decisions we cheat them of learning how to be responsible for when it really matters.

. . . .

See what happens when you say to your child,
'Don't do as you're told, but do as <u>you</u> decide.'

. . . .

Saskia learned to go to bed in good time

Saskia fought bedtimes. Always had. It felt like a battle of wills – she never went up to bed easily or early. Her parents had tried everything: baths, sitting on her bed chatting with her, cajoling, threatening . . . Then her mum's shift work changed to nights and suddenly Saskia found herself with no one to fight over what time she should go up to bed. At first she stayed up watching stuff on her computer till the small hours but that didn't last long as she felt the effects all the next day. When she was no longer being told what to do, Saskia began to take herself off to bed in time to have enough sleep.

A parent's wish

Every day of parenting can feel like a test in letting go: allowing the person who is my child to be who she is and not who I imagine her to be, or want her to be, or feel she ought to be.

Here's what I need to remember:
- My dreams for her are not her dreams. My opinions are not her opinions.
- I want the best for her but so often that can be *my* idea of what that best is.
- She speaks and I think I listen; but do I really hear?
- In so many ways, every day, she is showing me who she is. Yet sometimes I believe that to parent is to mould and influence her, rather than to pay proper attention to who she already is.
- I know how powerful a parent's judgement can be. I don't want her to be defined by mine.
- I don't want to fight who my child actually is. I want to dare to let her be.

I know my part in this is to:
- Be a good role model – example is one of the most powerful tools when parenting.
- Follow my own dreams.
- Pay attention and be guided by my feelings.
- Be myself.

When I give myself permission to create a life I love, respect my own thoughts and feelings, like my own body, wholeheartedly love the people around me, and have fun, then my daughter might be inspired to do the same.

But she will do it in her own way, and I want to let her.

WHOSE LIFE IS IT ANYWAY?

High heels, make-up, boys, staying out later, or myriad other changes may challenge us as our girls seek to feel more grown-up. All teenagers want to know that they are not the children they used to be; they want to know it for themselves and they want us to acknowledge it too. (Of course, sometimes they behave exactly like the child they once were and want all the allowances made for children!).

. . . .

How does a girl know she is becoming a woman in our culture? Her looks, her peers, her freedoms, her responsibilities, her self-perception . . . and ours.

. . . .

There are many markers that help to show your daughter's transition to womanhood: menarche, a romantic relationship, a driving test, leaving home, and many other smaller signposts. Especially if the importance of these markers is recognised within her circle of family and friends, she is less likely to look for other, riskier ways to confirm her progress.

The teenage years are a time to experiment, and this will test parents. We have to allow our children to choose different values, have different opinions and make different choices from ours.

. . . .

We step back, but we don't step down.

. . . .

There will still be some things that you stand firm on, and issues where limits can be negotiated. Look for that delicate balance between wanting to pass on the information that informs your values and not placing undue pressure on your teen to make the same choices that you would. And make every effort not to preach or persuade – that's the hard part for me. Parenting a teen is delicate work.

Samantha's mother guides her discreetly

Third of three girls, Samantha felt impatient to grow up. She watched her older sisters getting ready to go out at the weekends and wanted to go with them. Once they'd left, she'd sometimes creep into their rooms and have a go with their make-up. Some of the popular girls at school were starting to wear mascara, so Samantha 'borrowed' her sister's. Soon heavy eye-liner and lip gloss were added to what was considered cool at school. Samantha's mum saw her little girl setting off in the mornings looking more like a fashion model than a pupil. She understood Samantha's desire to fit in with the in-crowd at school, but she also felt that she was heading in the wrong direction. Instead of criticising or banning the make-up, Samantha's mum booked them both in for a free make-up session at their local department store. First she asked the make-up artist to show Samantha how to paint her face as if for a glamorous evening. Over the top, very dramatic, lots of fun. The photos were striking. Next Samantha was taught how to apply make-up for every day, very subtle, suitable for her age and skin tone. These photos were stunning. When Samantha showed both sets of photos to her friends and family, everyone favoured the more natural ones. Without her mother saying a thing Samantha toned down her daily cosmetics use.

Nurturing a good relationship with money

For some people money is an important part of how they define themselves, and a lot of youngsters have big ideas about how they'd like money to feature in their adult lives. There are many influences at play: how you are as a family with money, whether you have enough, how rich your daughter's friends are, what she sees in the media, the people she aspires to be like, her feelings when she sees people in poverty, her community spirit, your government's policies, your culture's attitude to wealth...

How do you help your daughter have a healthy relationship with money?

Discuss with her who has control over the money in your home. Who earns it? Who spends it? Who saves? How is money managed? Is it spoken about, or kept private? Is the family living within their means? Is there enough money? Is money fun, worrying, appreciated, scarce? The answers to these questions will tell you something about what you are teaching your children about money. Their observations of how money is spent and saved, controlled and enjoyed have long-reaching effects on how they will approach money. If you want to teach good money management, check first how you manage your own.

Society, peers and advertising all create expectations, but home sets a powerful example. You can live in a materialistic culture and still raise children who treasure what they have, who do not constantly yearn for more, who do their chores because it contributes to family life instead of expecting to be paid for doing them, who have their pocket money assured no matter what their behaviour, and who have an understanding of what their family is able to afford. There are studies into the 'over-justification effect' showing that paying children demotivates them.[1] And evidence that demonstrates that punishing children also demotivates them. Research supports the idea that strong, respectful, communicative relationships between parent and child give children the strongest sense of their self-worth and motivation.[2]

• •

Most fond childhood memories arise from spending time with your child, not from spending money.

• •

1. Harry L. Hom, Jr., 'Can you predict the overjustification effect?', *Teaching of Psychology*, 21 (1994), 36–7.
2   Alfie Kohn, 'The Risks of Rewards', *ERIC Digest* (1994). https://www.alfiekohn.org/article/risks-rewards/

Respecting her untidiness

The mess, the smell, the dirty clothes and plates in her room – are they our concern? Do we have the right to insist that they're sorted? After all, 'We pay the mortgage, we own the room!' I just want my teen's room clean and tidy. In fact, I'd like my whole house to be clean and tidy (where are the elves when you need them?) Sometimes it feels like my life is ebbing away in trying to keep our home in some sort of order, so when the chaos in my teen's room threatens to spill out through the door and down the stairs, I despair.

I have all manner of justifications for why a messy room must be sorted:

- It's unhygienic – mould on plates and damp socks are not healthy to sleep with.
- You will enjoy being in your room so much more once it's tidy.
- Clear room: clear thinking; they've researched and proved it.
- Dirty clothes have to be put in the basket, or they won't be washed.
- Clean clothes must be put away, or they'll get muddled with the dirty ones.
- I don't want to see all the mess every time I walk past your room.
- You won't have to waste time looking for lost things.
- You need to get into good habits.
- At least air the bed and open the curtains!
- You just can't live like that!

But *I* lived like that as a teen. I am a tidy adult now – not big on dusting, but I like to keep things organised . . . And yet I remember that when I was a teen my room was a tip. Clothes strewn across the floor; sweaty sports gear in plastic bags in the corner; sweet wrappers, LPs (remember them?), homework and cosmetics scattered throughout. It wasn't an act of rebellion and I wasn't a slob; it just didn't bother me and didn't seem important. Sporadically I would blitz the room, but it never stayed clear for long.

. . . .

Maybe how a child chooses to keep her room is not a reflection of who she is or what she is to become. Maybe a child's room needs to be one place that she can truly have things her way.

. . . .

A neat and tidy room does not necessarily mean a happy, sorted teen.

A messy and dirty bedroom does not indicate a lazy, slovenly teen.

My daughter's room often seems chaotic to me, but she says it feels creative.

When I respect that our children's rooms are their spaces to keep as they please, the tone of our conversations about their rooms changes. I may offer to help tidy up, and we spend a companionable hour chatting and rearranging. They may experience how much better it feels, and we discuss how to keep it that way. Even when it reverts back, if I respect that it's their room and their mess, we're all happier.

And here's a secret upside to our teen's messy room: she is more likely to be downstairs with us than disappearing upstairs to a bedroom in disarray.

Shannon's mum stopped nagging her about her room

Shannon and her mum were often at odds with each other – the state of Shannon's room was just one in a long stream of issues.

*Shannon: 'My mum hates me. She hates the way I dress, the way I eat, the way I behave, my friends – she hates everything about me. I can't get anything right with her, so I'm not going to try any more. It's my life! What gives her the right to tell me what to wear? She even has a go at me about my room – **my** room. What's it to her? None of her business, that's what. My room's the only place in the whole house where I can be me, and* *she wants to come in and order me to keep it how she wants it. She's got the rest of the house – why can't she leave me alone? It's like she's looking for things to have a go at me about. Bet she just wishes I didn't live there any more – that's it, that's what she wants: me out of her life!'*

Mum: 'I don't know what to do. Shannon and I used to be so close, but now all we do is clash. I'm on my own with her and you'd expect now she's older she'd help out a bit more. But she only thinks of herself and she is such hard work. Everything I say seems to rub her up the wrong way – it feels like I'm walking on eggshells with her. I wish we could go back to how it used to be.'

Things did change for Shannon and her mum, but it was gradual. A surprise gift helped: Shannon's mum was given a beautiful glass sand timer. It began as a joke one evening when her mum said in jest, 'Right, I'll never say another word about your room if you help me tidy up down here every night for the time it takes the sand to go down.' Shannon took her up on the challenge and there was something companionable that grew as they tidied together for ten minutes at the end of each evening. Her mum saw how much better they got on when she stopped nagging Shannon about her room.

Letting her manage her own time

We parents have opinions about how our children should spend their time. Too much time in their bedrooms, in the bathroom, lazing in bed, out with friends, shopping, hanging around doing nothing. Not enough time spent sleeping, exercising, helping, studying, being with family. No wonder they can't wait to grow up so they can choose to spend their time how they want! Nobody likes to be told what to do, least of all teens.

Our anxiety drives our nagging: fear that she will stay in bed all day and become a slob, get into the habit of rushed homework, never learn to cook, or do something she can't undo. If you want to influence your child's choices, try modelling behaviour rather than dictating, cajoling or bribing. What she sees you doing has a big impact. Make wise choices for yourself and then find ways for her to experience the benefits for herself:

- If you want her to get to bed earlier, offer to run her a bath and don't stay up late yourself.
- If you want her to exercise, take her ice-skating or to a pitch 'n' putt, borrow a dog to walk or do something else she'd want to repeat.
- If you want her to stay at the table for family meals, offer to be her sous-chef if she will make the meal, and then she is likely to insist everyone sits up to appreciate her efforts.
- If she rarely talks to you, give her your full attention when she does, and bite your tongue on any judgements.
- If all her clothes end up on her floor-drobe, offer to help her to find solutions, with a willingness to buy her a dirty-clothes basket, extra hangers, inventive storage.

Nagging just doesn't work. The better my relationship is with a child, the more likely she is to be sociable, up for doing new things and willing to help out. Whenever I'm all steamed up and irritated I try to remind myself to 'put the relationship first' and look for a kinder, more creative way of tackling things with my teen.

Teen screen time – off and out!

The benefits of being computer literate are obvious, but much has been written about the harmful effects on our children of too much gaming, texting, social media, streaming and surfing. I favour the big outdoors as entertainment, but then some of my best times as a child were scented with the smell of fresh-cut grass. I prefer my children off screens and outdoors because I want freedom for them. Freedom to roam away from home, to explore the world and play games of their own making, to take risks and to gather the sort of precious memories that childhood can be made of.

At a talk by Sue Palmer, the author of *Toxic Childhood*, we were asked to recall a favourite childhood memory of play. When we were asked whether that memory was outdoors, every single hand was raised. Whether there was no adult supervision, again all hands. When asked if it involved any manufactured toy (aside from a bicycle, which Sue described as a means of escaping adult supervision), not a single hand was raised. Finally, Sue asked if our children regularly had this kind of freedom. Very few of us were able to say yes. I am saddened to think that many of our children are being cheated of those play experiences that we chose as our best.

I remember that when my mother needed a break she would shunt us outside. We knew that if we were bored it was up to us to create our own diversions. We dreamed up the most amazing games, and, yes, they were sometimes inspired by the programmes we watched on television, but in adapting them we made them ours. We learned what happens if you don't test a tree branch before giving it your whole weight, and we learned what happens if you disable the brakes before a downhill bike race. We worked out how to make things fair, taught the only-child to share, and tested the limits of friendship. We looked out for the little ones (mostly), and we knew the smell and taste of the earth because, hey, it was a dare.

How often now do screens take the place of the big outdoors to give parents a break and occupy children? With our busy roads, and newspapers full of child abuse, it feels safer to keep our children within our own four walls. But what are we denying a daughter by logging her on rather than shunting her out? And is the worldwide web so very much safer than the outside world?

Staying safe on the web

The online world is constantly evolving, and our children are often at the frontier of this expansion. Our little pioneers should not be out adventuring ill-equipped. It's not realistic to be constantly at their side, so we adults want to teach them how to protect themselves, and to help them to understand why they would want to. This is best started young. And not done by giving a list of rules. Engage your child in figuring out how to stay safe, to help her see the dangers, and motivate her to want to protect herself.

Children come with natural inbuilt curiosity. What is porn? Why should I pause gaming when I'm nearly at level forty-five? Everyone's on Instagram – what's the problem? So what if a video of our drinking game gets onto Facebook? Why shouldn't I post my selfie taken at the local park?

Inform yourself so that you can guide your children.

My challenge with teens and technology is that it turns me into the 'screen police' in my own home, bringing tension to my relationships with my children. Over the years, our family has come up with some ingenious ways of alleviating screen-time tension, but, as so often happens with children, you devise a solution to a problem, you implement it and it works – for a while; but then the children change, the problem changes and you need a new solution.

When our teenagers were little, it was simple: we barely had any screen time, and toys provided an easy diversion. As the children grew older, we parents grew slacker, and anyway more screen time was appropriate. As the teen years approached, so grew the cries of 'It's not fair! Other kids can watch as much as they like'. When children are not studying or taking part in an organised activity, their desire to play seems to evaporate and be replaced by an urgent need to Snapchat, game or watch telly. They are all doing it. In homes across the land, what are we to do about all the hours spent on Xbox and YouTube? It's not all bad, but too much of it is. The challenge of the teen years is that our children want to be the boss of how they pass time, coupled with an enticing online culture. We are faced with a quandary: what is best for our children – to fit in and feel normal, or to live more healthily? Every family has to find the balance that works best for them.

The tussles over screen time do little for family harmony, so here's what I'm learning – learning slowly, because some part of my brain still thinks that announcing 'Too much screen' to a room of faces lit by the glow of some device will be all it takes for them to log off. Rather than focusing on what I don't want, I'm concentrating on what I do want. I have discovered that when we have our meals outside, we often linger in the garden together. When I'm my children's taxi driver, they can have their choice of music in exchange for no mobiles. One holiday, I started to read out loud the book I was so enjoying and soon I had the whole family settling down every evening for another chapter. On our way back from football I take my daughter to the café, and we chat. I help her untangle the mess in her costume jewellery box while telling her stories about me and her grandma as young girls. When I give time to each child, they will often carry on with that activity after I leave them for the cooking pot or the paperwork mountain – or today to go back to my screen to write this!

CHAPTER FIVE

Her changing relationships

In adolescence your daughter's body changes, her sensitivity changes and so do her relationships. Parents no longer seem perfect, friendship groups disintegrate, social media takes hold and romance rocks her world. In this chapter, I will discuss how you can support her in having healthy friendships and happy romance, as well as the importance of the loving influence of her family. There is a section about social media that provides ideas for how to befriend this powerful influence in your teen's life while recognising dangers such as pornography; and a Girl Talk section provides answers to the questions about romance that preteens and teens ask most frequently in Girls Journeying Together. Finally, I explain the power of family mealtimes and family meetings as essential tools to continue strengthening your relationship with your daughter.

FRIENDS, BELONGING AND SOCIAL MEDIA

At first parents are everything. Your baby girl needed you for love and warmth, food and fun. You introduce her to family and friends, and to begin with she will play alongside other children before gradually learning how to play *with* them. She learns how to be caring and the importance of sharing. Hopefully you also show her how to stand up for herself. It's a balance: you want your daughter to be nice but not *too* nice. You want her to have good social skills but not lose touch with herself.

Many mothers feel they've been trained to please others at the expense of expressing their own needs, so they have to be careful not to pass this on to their daughters.

Children watch us to see how we are with our friends and what our friendships mean to us. They will also be keen to see how we behave when we don't get on well with someone. You are your daughter's touchstone: she looks to your example for how to behave and what to hold important. You, your relations and your friends are her role models.

Your daughter's friendships intensify as she heads towards her teens. This often coincides with increased access to social media and being more exposed to cultural influences, celebrity values and social pressures. Around this time nature also kicks in and her brain enters a period of change. Throughout her teens she feels the drama of life's ups and downs more acutely, becomes more spontaneous and less considered and has a tendency to align herself with her peers. This is a critical time when she needs your guidance more than ever, but she needs it offered in a different way. She needs to feel you relating to her as you would to someone who is no longer a young child. If you can find more mature ways to be connected, she won't want to distance herself from you even though some of her peers distance themselves from their parents. You can keep your role as key mentor in her life. She can be influenced by her peers while not being ruled by them.

We all experience peer pressure, but teens are most prone to suffering from the force of it. They need us to respect how powerful it feels to them and not mock them for the times when they succumb. Instead you can help your daughter to figure out when it's okay just to go with the crowd and when to stand firm for what she believes in. You want the authority in her life to pass from you to her – and not via her peers. Parents have the ability to put the needs of their child ahead of their own – her friends won't be doing that. No one cares for her as you do – and if she knows that, she will continue to come to you when she needs help.

It takes effort to stay in close connection with your daughter as she heads for her teens. She can seem to need you less, especially as she is with her friends more, and it's tempting for you to take the opportunity to take up salsa dancing, socialise more or do whatever you have been waiting to have free time for. It's great for her to see you following your passions, but don't drop the baby now. Teens still need their parents to be around, keeping an eye, being there to listen to injustices and hurt feelings, providing food!

You know best how to maintain your connection with your daughter. Do stuff together that she enjoys. Listen to her, be interested and involved. And it's never too late to win her back if the connection has slipped – but, as discussed in Chapter One, that takes more drastic action.

Your daughter's friendships are powerfully important. These people are going to journey towards adulthood with her, adventuring, commiserating and celebrating with her. Together they will learn about companionship, trust, secrets, betrayal, meanness, kindness, empathy, exclusion and cliques, diplomacy, loyalty, reliability, affection, confiding, small talk, gossip, status, copying, liking, mocking, snitching, respect, difference and so much more. Your daughter will learn how to cope when people are horrible and come to discern which friends are true friends. This will be useful her whole life.

A reminder to hang on to old friends. In the social turmoil of moving to senior school many girls lose touch with their childhood friends. In the first flush of romance many girls forsake their best mates. Help your daughter to maintain her connection with the people who know her well and hold some of the stories of her past, as it will help her to hold on to her sense of self in her teenage years. It's good for her to learn that she can have a variety of friendships, each meeting different needs, and overall giving her a network of support as she grows up.

What does it take to belong?

'Why can't our family just be like everyone else?'
'If you come to pick me up, don't wear that hat.'

'I just want to be normal.'

The cry of many a teenager! They strive for uniformity. But they also want to feel unique.

Feeling more self-aware than ever often makes a teen not want to stand out. At the same time they crave the affirmation that special attention brings. It's confusing: 'I want to be me – but I want that me to be like everyone else.'

Children feel the pressure to conform: they want to fit in at school and at home and still be their own person. It's impossible for a child to be like her friends *and* as the school wishes her to be *and* comply to family expectations – *and* still discover who she is.

Fitting in isn't the same as belonging. Fitting in is tying yourself into knots to try to be what you imagine others want you to be. You lose yourself. Belonging is being yourself first and then discovering who you like to hang out with and what you enjoy doing, while still being yourself. The most powerful way to teach this to our children is to live it ourselves, or at least try to.

You gain a sense of belonging when you let people see who you really are. You can only do this if you believe that you are acceptable as you are – with all your faults, strengths and quirky habits. If our children don't believe themselves to be okay just as they are, then they are prone to try to fashion themselves into something other than their true selves. This can continue their whole lives. If childhood is spent feeling chastised, criticised, guided and shaped, then children believe that they must change to become acceptable. In response, some children draw inside and seem to comply, while others rebel; both these reactions are acts of self-preservation, but neither leads to a true expression of self. Both hurt. When these children grow up they continue this process by being self-critical or oppositional. If either of these was your experience as a child, your impulse in turn will be to try to shape your children.

. . . .

Children need us to respect who they actually are and not try to change them. They need us to champion their individuality.

. . . .

Jade learns to be herself

Jade has mild cerebral palsy, so she's not too steady on her feet and she has learning support in the classroom. Her parents worked hard for her to be in a mainstream school where she had a nice bunch of friends, and she was managing okay. Then it all changed. The move to secondary school was hard for her – suddenly there were kids who made fun of the way she walked, and some of her friends became self-conscious about being seen with her. Jade became obsessed with getting the right clothes, the right haircut, the right bag in an attempt to be accepted. She flew into a rage when the shirt her mum bought her had the wrong shape collar. She campaigned for a better phone. She just wanted to be like the others. It was when she begged to be allowed to go to a rollerblading party, even though she'd never be able to rollerblade safely, that her parents sat her down and had a really hard talk with her. In some ways she would never be like her friends. Some things she'd never be able to join in. But trying to look like them and do everything they were doing wasn't the way to be included. She needed to be herself, fiercely herself, and then see who were her true friends.

Do you want your daughter to stand up for herself?

'Yes! Well, mostly, as long as it doesn't mean that she refuses to tidy her room!'

We want our girls to be able to say 'No!' when they need to and to go for what they really want in life. Teens find this particularly hard, despite how well they seem to do this at home! Girls experience a lot of pressure to please. As parents we have the challenge of raising girls who think for themselves, who listen to themselves, and who have the courage to do what is right for them, despite conflicting influences from friends, teachers, parents and society.

So, while you may wish for your daughter to do as you say and follow your good advice, really what you want is a daughter who does what *she* thinks is right for her and follows that.

Hopefully your daughter is acquainted with a woman or two who lives true to herself and knows her own mind. The most effective way of raising a girl who will stand up for herself is for her to see you standing up for *yourself*. Every time you do, it will be easier for her to do so too.

Social media – befriend this powerful force

Imagine your home wasn't your own, you couldn't go where you pleased and your days were spent in a place where you weren't really free to speak. Then imagine someone handed you a magical device that kept you in touch with your friends, delivered useful information, took photos, played music and videos and provided endless entertainment. What's not to like?

The internet and social media are compelling. They offer a great deal and promise more. Girls seek comfort and companionship there. They seek answers to the questions, 'Who am I?' 'Do you like me?' 'Am I alone?' 'What is the answer to my geography homework?' They find a kind of connection that is constantly available. They find stimulation and diversion too. They also find pressure to be constantly accessible, pictures they'd be better off not seeing, and people who are nasty. There's a downside to most things.

Our job is to help them to take advantage of the good and avoid the bad.

Teach your daughter how to make the most of this medium, while keeping herself healthy and safe, and start the conversation young. You can't be over her shoulder the whole time, so she is going to need to understand *why* it's important to stay internet-healthy and cyber-safe, as well as *how* to do so. Go online and learn about how to guide your child to avoid the current dangers: common sense like not giving out personal details; setting privacy and tagging settings; disabling geolocation; not being unkind; handling cyber-nastiness; watching out for people pretending to be someone they are not; never meeting in person anyone she meets online; remembering that everything she posts exists forever for anyone to find. Learn what platforms she is using so you can help her to understand the benefits and pitfalls. Encourage her to notice how she feels when she is on social media – when does it buoy her up, when does it bring her down? Talk with her about how the fear of missing out might make it hard to switch off, yet there's great value in having downtime. While being internet literate is an essential skill, so is being able to be alone with her thoughts. Remind her to keep a realistic perspective. Life isn't really how it looks on Facebook – people post their best moments, they photoshop their images, and number of likes isn't a measure of worth. Ask her where it's easy to be herself on the internet and when it's not possible. Find out whether she has ever come across something she didn't want to see, and what she did then. Or if she has ever been part of an online drama that was made worse because the communication was not face-to-face. Muse about how life would look if none of us had access to social media. Wonder if she has ever cheated sleep because of the allure of the next text or YouTube clip. See if she will friend you on her media platforms so that you can keep a very discreet eye – but never comment or engage.

Hardest of all, notice your own example. Do you put your phone out of earshot at mealtimes and bedtime? Do you turn to the internet when you are bored? Do you substitute socialising in person with relating online? Do you turn the wifi off at ten and do something else before bed? Is your online persona very different from your offline one? Do you turn off when you notice that your internet time is not making you feel okay? Do you stick to family agreed rules for social media yourself?

Young people generally like it when you try to engage with their world, especially when you allow them to be expert guides. Doing this will help you to work together at finding the right balance between your daughter's online and offline life.

Leah and her mother reach a compromise on internet use

Leah and her parents were always at odds over her screen time. She texted at the table, stayed up late watching YouTube clips, kicked off if there wasn't wifi on holiday, and wouldn't be parted from her phone. She took selfies at every opportunity, had become obsessed with how she looked, and often got upset by the texts that flew back and forth. Her parents were worried about her. Yet every time they tried talking to her it became a battle between them accusing her of being antisocial, and her fighting for her right to 'have a life'. Their arguments got nowhere until something happened that really rattled Leah. One of her friends was badly bullied online and resorted to taking an overdose. Leah told her mum – and this turned into a bigger conversation about all the pressures to measure up, to sort out text misunderstandings, to be online active and to get 'likes'. Her mum showed Leah a website offering social media guidance to teens. This was the beginning of a much more respectful conversation that gradually brought a healthy change to Leah's internet use.

Amara's mum was out of her depth

Amara's mum didn't understand phones, computers or any of that stuff, but she could see that it was important for her daughter to have a phone to keep in touch with her friends and everything else that was out there. She asked other mums whether there was anything she should know and was a bit overwhelmed by all the advice and different opinions. So she went to her local youth leader, who offered to talk to Amara and her mum together so that they could figure out if there needed to be any rules and what to watch out for.

BIRDS AND BEES TANGLED IN THE WEB

Online porn is a big worry and we all need to protect our children. Women on television are sexier than ever before. In magazines they reveal ever more, and what they reveal is increasingly perfect. Online, well, online anything goes. Any child on the web is only two clicks away from adult pornography and many do inadvertently come into contact with explicit images at a young age. The average age of first exposure in the UK is eleven years, and a study in one local authority found that by the age of thirteen 50 per cent of girls and 100 per cent of boys had accessed online porn.[1] Many of these girls said they were pressurised to look at pornography by the boys.

. . . .

Online pornography becomes sex education for many children, and it's influencing their expectations about early romance.

. . . .

Access is easy, but the quality is dubious. Online porn is graphic, degrading and often violent against women. Pornography distorts our children's views on relationships, violence and gender roles. It shapes boys' expectations of girls and the female body.[2] It damages body image. It confuses young people's understanding of consent and enjoyable sexual behaviour. It can become a compulsion. Unfortunately, the problem can be invisible to parents. Children want somewhere quiet to do their homework, requiring a computer that often ends up in their bedrooms, which makes their access to online pornography difficult to monitor and problematic to restrict. Safety filters may solve the problem for our youngest ones, but older children are adept at circumventing filters,

1   Elena Martellozzo et al., '"I wasn't sure it was normal to watch it": the impact of online pornography on the values, attitudes, beliefs and behaviours of children', Middlesex University/ NSPCC (2016, revised May 2017). https://www.nspcc.org.uk/services-and-resources/research-and-resources/2016/i-wasnt-sure-it-was-normal-to-watch-it/
2   https://www.ippr.org/files/publications/pdf/young-people-sex-relationships_Aug2014.pdf

and smartphones go with them everywhere. The European Parliament considered banning online porn. Iceland is banning it by filtering at source. The UK government decided not to.

Increasingly prevalent is peer-to-peer content, generated by teens and shared between them. Sexting – sending sexually explicit messages or photographs – is commonplace despite being illegal for under eighteens. For many young people sexting is fun and they see no harm in it, but some girls report being placed under pressure by boyfriends to send photos of themselves, and sometimes those photos are then shared around the school.

Children need our help to navigate this virtual new world. Their curiosity is natural. We mustn't make them feel wrong for being inquisitive, but they also need to know the risks and the harmful effects, how to resist peer pressure, and alternative ways to find out what they are curious to know. Keep yourself up to date so that you can guide your daughter.

The best kind of filtering is not software but human, where your daughter checks in with a trusted adult or older teen who helps her to learn how to self-regulate her exposure. Ultimately, it's got to be your daughter who keeps her internet use healthy and safe.

Meanwhile, don't be afraid to turn your wifi off at night!

BOYFRIENDS, GIRLFRIENDS AND NON-BINARY FRIENDS

Many parents hold back from talking about romance with their children because they don't want to spoil their innocence. Trouble is, if you haven't talked about relationships with your daughter as she grows up, neither of you will be comfortable to have those conversations when she is older. Also, her naivety will make her vulnerable. It's never too late, though, so just brace yourself and get the conversation started.

Opportunities to talk arise all the time: when you see a young couple kissing, when the news is full of an LGBT Pride march, or when you hear of a teen pregnancy. These can be ideal times to ask your daughter what she thinks and share what you know. If you sound judgemental, she is less likely to risk talking to you. Over the years, I've learnt that children are naturally curious about lots of things, including sex, but they will only ask if you seem cool about it. I've also learnt to keep my answers short and see if they ask for more. It's easy to over-explain and give information they are not ready for. Say just a little and wait; children will often go away and think about what they have learnt and come back later with another question if they want to know more.

'Where does the baby come from?' is not necessarily asking for a lecture on intercourse and labour. 'It grows inside the Mummy's belly' might be enough. Or another question may follow: 'How does it get in there?' – in which case you might answer, 'Well, a baby starts to grow when the daddy's seed joins up with the mummy's egg.' A year can pass before a question like 'How does the seed get to the egg?' can be answered with 'Well, the mummy and daddy get very close and cuddly and then the daddy gives his seed, called sperm, to the Mummy,' or 'How does the baby get out?' and 'Through a hole between the mummy's legs.' It's good to reassure a child that children can't have babies, and from there one day will come the conversation about periods.

If your parents never talked to you about sex, you may need to practise first by talking with other mums about what they say to their children. That way you become used to talking openly before broaching the subject with your daughter. If your child chooses not to confide in you, it doesn't mean you have failed: some people are just more private than others; but you need to give off an air of availability and acceptance, just in case she does ever want to talk something through. Parents fear that talking about sex with their children will make them more likely to have sex earlier, but actually the opposite is true. Otherwise it will be music videos, films, friends and YouTube that teach your daughter, and that's never going to be the healthiest way for her to learn.

Girl Talk – About relationships

In this section you will find answers to questions that preteens and teens regularly ask me during sessions of Girls Journeying Together.

How do you get a boyfriend or girlfriend?

Think of it like starting a friendship. You notice that you like someone and you find ways to get to know them better by talking to them, spending time with them, sussing out if they like you too. Body language speaks volumes, so notice what you communicate to one another without talking. Eye contact tells you a lot and so does the way someone responds when you smile at them.

How is it different from just being friends?

Often you feel hyper-aware of the other person, tingly and excited and nervous when you see them. You'll want to be close to that person, not just physically but mentally and emotionally too. It's natural that you'll want to impress them, and that can make it hard to relax and be yourself, but in the long run you want to be with someone who likes you for who you are, whatever you're wearing, doing or saying. It's exhausting to be in a relationship with someone you feel you have to make an effort to please – it's not 'you' who is in the relationship then.

What happens on a date?

The point of a date is to enjoy each other's company, so neither of you should do anything you don't want to. It could be that you meet in a café, go to see a film. You might go for a wander and then get something to eat, go swimming or bowling or listen to music. Do something that you both enjoy. Then if you feel comfortable you might hold hands, cuddle or kiss. Being physical together is for when you feel safe and close to that person. This is entirely up to you and it's important to wait until you both feel ready. There's often pressure to hurry this bit up, but don't – take your time and enjoy it. And much as it's nice to have a girlfriend or boyfriend, lots of people in their twenties have never been on a date, so wait until you meet someone special.

How do you know if someone is right for you?

The same things that make a good friend make a good boyfriend or girlfriend. If you like someone to be funny, friendly, kind, honest, caring and adventurous, then that's what you'll enjoy in a romantic friendship. If you like people who are sporty, bookish, musical or arty, you'll find that appealing in a romance too. You need to have enough in common to enjoy talking together. You will want to be able to trust the other person with your secrets and your dreams, your highs and your lows. And then you want to find that person physically appealing. Quite often when you first get interested in someone, you might find that you feel jittery whenever you see them, excited but nervous, warm and quivery and getting a bit obsessed by your feelings for them. That's normal.

What if you're asked out and you're not sure?

You will know when it's a definite yes, and it's lovely when it's that clear. Sometimes it's a definite no, and that's awkward, but look for a kind way to say so. Keep it simple; they don't want to hear lots of explanations that sound like excuses. Help them not to lose face, by finding something genuine and nice to say, and don't turn them down in front of other people. Get back to normal with them as soon as you can afterwards – don't avoid them. Don't go around telling lots of people that they asked you and you refused them. And don't say yes out of pity or because you haven't the courage to say no – it'll be much harder to get out of it later.

Then there are the times when you're really not sure. It's fine to suggest hanging out together with a group of friends first. Perhaps it's your nerves at being asked out that make you want to say no; remember that it's just someone suggesting that you get to know each other better because they like you – you don't have to want to marry them! But listen to your gut feeling: a not sure can sometimes really be a no.

How do I know if I'm gay?

You will just know. Most people feel attracted to people of the opposite gender, but lots of people enjoy same-gender relationships. These days we understand that there's lots of different ways of expressing sexuality – you might have heard of some: heterosexual, homosexual, transsexual, bisexual, asexual, pansexual. It can be daunting if you find yourself in a minority, so seek out other people who share your preference to give you the confidence to know that you're okay however you are.

What age do people have sex?

There's lots of different ways to be physically close and express your affection for someone. Trust your body to tell you what feels good and what doesn't. If we use the word 'sex' to mean sexual intercourse, the average age for the first experience is eighteen in the UK and the USA and it ranges from fifteen to twenty-four across the world. Average age means that a lot of people are much older than that the first time, and also a lot of people are younger. There's no 'right' age. Different countries around the world have a legal age when heterosexual sex is allowed, which ranges from eleven to twenty-one, and in some countries sexual relations are forbidden outside marriage.

First make sure you know about safe sex – how to enjoy sex without catching any diseases or getting pregnant. Don't get drunk and have sex that you regret later. Some young people feel under pressure to be sexually active and find it easier to be (or pretend to be) drunk. Trust your body to guide you in how to make it pleasurable. Make your first time memorable in a good way.

What is consent?

It's important to make sure that you and your partner feel okay about anything you do together. You can check this out by asking, 'Is this okay?' If there is any doubt, for either of you, then stop. It's never okay to guilt someone, make them feel like they owe it, ignore them pulling away or give them a hard time for not wanting to do something that you want to do.

What is porn?

Porn (pornography) is pictures or films that are made to be sexually exciting. It's natural to be curious, especially as it's kept away from children. There are some problems with porn, however: it gives you wrong ideas of what sex is really like, it can be hard to get the pictures out of your head, it can become addictive, it messes with your ability to have real sex with a real person, and there's lots of porn that's violent and degrading towards women.

What is the difference between sex that isn't okay and sex that is fun?

Trust your instincts – if something doesn't feel right, then it's not right. It's not always easy to say no though, so don't feel ashamed. Find someone you really trust to help you out of this situation. You need to know that if ever you don't want to do something, or you change your mind halfway through, you always have the right to say, 'Stop!'

Sex that's fun – this is what to expect and aim for. It doesn't always go right, but hopefully you can laugh when it doesn't. Sex is adult play.

THE IMPORTANCE OF MOTHERS

Girls learn about the world and about becoming women from many sources: you, other women, girlfriends, boys, their dads, films, books, songs, popular media – but you are her main role model. She has grown up with you as her embodiment of womanhood. She will have observed you, heard what you have to say about your life as a woman, sensed how you feel about your body, witnessed how you manage your emotions and your needs, listened in on your conversations, felt your happiness, observed your strengths and noted your weaknesses, noticed how you relate to the world, and learnt what is important to you. Unconsciously, most adults still define themselves in relation to their parents – emulating them or making clear choices not to be like them. Parents are powerful! You can positively influence your daughter by modelling what you wish for her in how you live your life.

Forget telling her how you want her to be. Show her instead:

- If you want her to stand up for herself, stand up for yourself.
- If you want her to be more considerate, be more considerate towards her.
- If you want her to be reasonable, be more reasonable with her.
- If you want her to talk politely, talk politely to her.
- If you want her to help more, don't do everything yourself.
- If you want her to worry less about her looks, worry less about yours.
- If you want her to make the right choices, make the right choices for yourself.
- If you want her to withstand the influence of peers, withstand the pressure of others yourself.
- If you want her to look after herself, look after yourself.

. . . .

Our children can bring out the very best in us.

. . . .

Nagging is ignored, and yelling drowns out the message. If you really want to influence your daughter's behaviour, be someone she respects and would want to emulate. This doesn't mean being how she wants you to be: it means being true to yourself.

Don't be fooled. Even when our teens appear not to care about what we think, they need our good opinion of them; they need our willingness to listen to their latest fascination; they need our faith that their lives will turn out okay. Remember the excruciating sensitivity of the teen years. We all want our parents to think well of us. No matter what our age, our parents' disapproval bothers us and their high regard encourages us. You are incredibly important to your teen and it is never too late to set an example through your own behaviour.

• •

The way you talk to your child becomes her inner voice.

• •

Reshaping the mother–daughter relationship

'Don't treat me like a child!'
'Well, don't behave like one then!'

Excitable, irascible, wanting to do everything for herself, resisting going to bed – are there moments with your teenager that are reminiscent of her toddler days? Both are times of transition when her natural maturation requires that she ventures away from you. Paradoxically, she needs you there more – to push away from, and to come back to.

> *It's odd – I'm having to take care of my teenager more rather than less. Whereas a year ago she could be relied upon in the mornings to sort herself out, now I find myself having to help with breakfast, check she takes what she needs for the day, and clock-watch to ensure she leaves on time.*
>
> *Karen, mother to a sixteen-year-old*

There is good reason for this shift. The bit of the brain that has a lot to do with organisation, decision-making and sound judgement is being remodelled. It's a highly adaptive period, ideally suited to teens figuring out who they are, what is important to them, in which direction they wish to head, and for moving away from the safety of home into the complicated outside world. Teens need more help with everyday tasks than they did before. They need babying while simultaneously needing to feel their growing independence.

> *I worried that if I stepped back in, providing the kind of care that was needed in much earlier years, it would leave my teen incapable. Now I'm cherishing the intimacy of it. Somehow, while so disorganised and disorientated, she's more open to my ministrations ... There'll come a day when she's grown and gone and I'll remember these chaotic mornings with fondness.*
>
> *Karen, mother to a sixteen-year-old*

If this can be treated as a blessing rather than a chore, then it's an opportunity to stay connected during the teen years. Many mothers who returned to work after their children started school find themselves needing to reduce their working hours in the teen years. Teens may appear to need us less, but actually they just need us in a different way – in a 'holding' way, providing a stable base from which to venture.

> *We're in the midst of exams and my teen wants me to back off. No gentle reminders to revise or advice on exam technique required, thank you very much. The same applies to nudges towards getting to bed at a reasonable time, eating sensibly, screen time or dressing appropriately for the weather. My teenager wants to take charge – unless it all becomes too much. Then suddenly I am needed to help with managing studies, to cook something nutritious, to remind about bed, to hold the hand of my teenage toddler. The speed at which we flip from 'Leave me to it!' to 'You have to help me!' can make my head spin. Just when I'm adjusting to loosening my grip on the tiller, persuading myself to trust that the right decisions will be made or the wrong ones learnt from, I'm called back on board to help steer the ship again.*
>
> *Karen, mother to a sixteen-year-old*

. . . .

The job of parenting a teen is like performing magic – to be there invisibly, offering support only when needed and without being seen to do so.

. . . .

It is worth remembering that your daughter loves you while she hates you – and you can love her while hating her behaviour. A stressed teen is stressful to be around, as she takes it out on everyone at home. If your daughter is struggling, she may not come to you for support but perhaps she will tell you that she needs help by how she behaves. Be someone she feels is on her side – who always looks for the best in her, seeks the real reason behind bad behaviour, and makes time to be with her no matter how she is behaving.

If not you, then who?

Even clever girls can get pregnant. Even aware girls get chlamydia. If parents are teaching their children, and teachers are covering this stuff in school, why the mistakes?

In my early twenties I was an outreach worker employed by schools and youth clubs to discover and cover any gaps in teen sex education. The level of the teenagers' knowledge was remarkable, but so was their inability to apply their knowledge to real life.

'I just get drunk and forget everything,' was a common plea.

'No way. You can't talk about condoms, not when you're just about to . . .' was another frequent remark.

Teenagers often lack the confidence and the communication skills to negotiate good sex, and use alcohol to get them through. So if we are really going to educate our children for healthy sexual encounters, it's not enough to cover the mechanics. Too often sex is taught as a reproductive biological act rather than a loving expression of intimacy between two people. Learning how to be discerning and to exercise choice, how to listen to the rise and fall of desire and understand our cyclical monthly rhythms are all more important than being instructed upon what goes where – that bit's easy.

Having a child is a life-changing event, as you well know, so if your daughter is sexually active and you fear that she is not taking responsibility for her fertility, you need to take drastic action. Take her to your local young mothers unit to meet teens who have babies. Get them to do the tough talking – and they will – describing to her the reality of life with a baby.

Talking about sex does not make it more likely to happen: forbidding and silence do. If we expect teens to find the courage and the skills to negotiate safe and enjoyable encounters, we must be willing to find the courage and the skills to talk to them about how they might do that – or find someone else who's comfortable teaching them. It's not just information that your daughter needs: it's help in finding the confidence and the words to insist on her own pleasure and a condom. Research shown by Anne-Marlene Henning and Tina Bremer-Olszweski in their book *Sex and Lovers: A Practical Guide* tells us that young people most want to learn about sex and relationships from their parents, despite the awkwardness;[3] so if chatting to your child about sex doesn't come naturally to you, draw on websites, books and television programmes.

We want to teach our children about the pleasure of sex. If our main message is about avoiding pregnancy and disease, we are just passing on our fears and not **teaching the most important thing about sex: that it is adult fun.**

---

3   Schools Health Education Unit, Exeter, 'Young People into 2013'. http://www.sheu.org.uk

> ### 'Back off, Mum!'
>
> Do not be fooled by our cultural belief, or your teen's belief, that her friends are more important to her than her parents. Good friends are a great support, but the love and care of parents is essential. The healthy impulse to separate in the teen years also creates feelings of anxiety for your teenager (and often for the parent too!), and she needs you to provide her with a solid base from which she can launch herself into her future.

Letter to a teen daughter

I have written this letter to encapsulate the complexity of the mother-daughter relationship through the teenage years. My hope is to give voice to motherly feelings that might not be easily expressed in the midst of conflict or distance in the relationship. However, the turmoil can still be held in love.

My darling girl

You are growing up, no longer my little girl, but always my precious child.

It's difficult being your mum right now because we clash so often and it feels like I keep getting it wrong for you. I'm not trying to ruin your life! You want me to back off, and I will, but just maybe it's slower than you want – partly because I'm doing what I think is right for you, and partly because I'm finding it hard to let go. Bear with me. I think you know that it will happen more swiftly if I can see you taking reasonably good care of yourself. I don't want to stand in your way, but I'm your mum and it's still my job to look out for you.

You're right, sometimes I don't trust you to make the right decisions, but that's not because I think you are untrustworthy, but because I know how hard it is to do the right thing when you're with a crowd, especially when there is alcohol around. One day you will be totally in charge of your own life, but while you are still getting there I'm sharing that role with you.

When you were a baby you needed me for everything. It was quite a shock to be so totally depended upon, but I loved being there for you, even at 4 a.m.! Now you're older and you need me in a different way, but you don't have to try not to need anything from me to prove that you are growing up. I'm still here for you, on your side. Sometimes our relationship is smooth and sometimes not – that's natural and it's okay. It's normal for you to resent me sometimes (and me to resent you!). We still love each other, even when it doesn't feel easy.

I'm glad that you have friends that mean so much to you. You're right, I don't really know what it's like to be a teen now, but don't forget that I love and care about you too and I do know some stuff about life that might be useful to you.

I want you to know how gorgeous you are. Gorgeous in who you are and in how you look. In some ways I don't even want to talk about how you look – there's too much emphasis on looks – but at the same time I see you worrying about it and I wish you could see yourself through my eyes: your smooth skin, clear eyes and gorgeous hair; the way you hold yourself, your long fingers (just like your grandmother's), and your funny baby toe (just like mine); your strong legs, olive colouring, the birthmark on your arm, and your soft belly. You are so beautiful, and you're so much more than what you look like. I want you to understand that you have a choice here: you can choose to view yourself with kind eyes and love what you see, or you can choose to look with unkind eyes and focus on what you don't like and yearn to be different. It's your choice. Not an easy choice, I know; so help yourself by not poring over magazines with their fake photos and measuring yourself against celebrities, or even against your friends. You are who you are. You are so very, very special.

I have confidence in you. Of course I waver sometimes, but deep down I know that your life will work out okay. You are already a wonderful person and are finding your own right way. Please know that I am cheering you on. (I'm sorry that it sometimes feels more like nagging.) You have your whole adult life ahead of you, and you have me, your biggest fan, wishing the very best for you.

Do you remember how, when you were little, I used to say, 'Love you always, forever, no matter what'? That's still true and it will never change. Just please take care of yourself as you grow; you are incredibly precious.

With all my love

Mum

Making moments to remember

We all have moments that we remember from childhood. Some are lovely memories, some are of times that were shocking or testing. Many are of simple little moments that you would never imagine would take special place in the gallery of your past. I remember stroking the purple velvet of my mother's evening dress while she sat on the edge of my bed. I remember leaping over a wide stream with my dad. My son remembers a midnight walk along our lane in the pitch black. What these fragments have in common is that there was something about the circumstances that called us utterly into the moment. That is what gave it magic.

Inhabiting the present moment is not always easy when we have our eye on the clock and much to squeeze into the day. However, notice the difference between brushing your daughter's hair in a hurry with your thoughts on what is next on the list, and brushing her hair while noticing the tug of the brush and the softness of her hair. Experiment with bringing this kind of attention to other everyday tasks that you engage in with your daughter. Be present with her. These are the things that will then form your cherished magical moments together.

DADS AND DAUGHTERS

A girl's relationship with her father influences all her future relationships with men.

Dads can show their daughters how to love, play, feel safe with a man, disagree, be in the world, debate, think, follow the rules, bend the rules, completely flout the rules, have fun and be loved. Dads show their daughters how a man expresses his feelings and how a man doesn't have to be perfect.

- How a father treats his daughter will shape how she expects to be treated by men.
- How her father treats her mother will shape how she expects to be treated by men.
- How her mother and father treat each other will give her a blueprint for how men and women relate.

Who are the significant men in your daughter's life? Dads and father figures have an important part to play – how they are with her will cast the model for what she expects from the men in her life. However, many dads feel unsure as their daughter enters puberty, not knowing how to relate to her. Your daughter may have always had a special bond with her dad, him wrapped around her little finger, and as she matures she can become quite flirtatious. She is just experimenting, and if he has the self-assurance to stay in close connection with her, he can validate her as an emergent woman. His job is to treasure and respect her. Dads who are fearful when their daughters are starting to date can protect them by treating them in the way that they want them to be treated by others. Dads who aim to have an honest, honourable, healthy relationship with their daughters create that expectation for all their daughters' other relationships. Dads matter.

BEYOND COMPARE – THE ROLE OF SIBLINGS

Having a brother or sister can be a source of great comfort: you grow up together, you have someone who knows what your childhood is like. It can also be a source of much conflict: with your siblings you learn about competition and sharing, standing up for yourself and fighting fair. A child's position in the family influences her character: whether the eldest, the youngest, the middle child or the only child, each has a distinctive experience within the same family, and something different to offer.

Children can be great allies, but we can unwittingly set them against each other. I made a promise to myself when I was pregnant with our second child to resist comparing our children with each other, even in my head. I didn't want our children to grow up defining themselves as 'more than' or 'less than' each other. Of course children will be aware of an older sibling who can run faster, or another sibling who sings beautifully, but actually children are often so busy being themselves that they don't naturally infect their thinking with comparisons – not unless we teach them to. The child who is less meticulous than a sibling and who is labelled careless or messy will become ever more careless and messy. The child who is dreamy and less thoughtful than a sibling, if labelled thoughtless is more likely to give up trying to be considerate. The child who is energetic and passionate may become ever more boisterous and noisy if labelled so, while a more sedate, reflective sibling if labelled lazy may become lazy. When we ascribe labels to children, they believe us, and the label becomes a self-fulfilling prophecy.

A child who is quietly told that she is the most generous of her siblings now has a terrible burden to carry. Not only must she now outgive her siblings to keep her position, but she also feels a sense of ill-ease remembering all her ungenerous thoughts or acts, alongside knowing all the times when her siblings have been generous. We all want our children to feel good about themselves, but not through competing with those they love and live with, and not at the expense of their relationship with their siblings.

Favouritism hurts. When an adult mis-exercises power by conferring a preference for one child over another, this encourages that child to base part of her sense of self on how she is perceived by that adult and then invest energy in retaining that position. Although the adult's misguided intention may be to bolster the child's self-confidence, it does the opposite.

If we want our children to be allies in the business of growing up, we need to avoid comparing them and setting them up as rivals. It's perfectly possible to communicate with each child without reference to their siblings.

'That was kind – you remembered that she can't eat nuts,' rather than, 'You're the kind one in this family. No wonder you have so many friends.'

'Hey, too loud! Take the volume down,' rather than, 'Why do I have to keep telling you to quiet down? The others don't need reminding.'

Siblings disagree and argue – it's hard learning to live alongside people; but if there's constant fighting this signals a deeper problem. Children naturally want the approval of the adults around them, so if their behaviour doesn't garner that approval we have to figure out what problem they are trying to solve. Children fight if they are not getting something they need. Stressed and time-poor parents juggling the needs of home and work often find that their children fighting is a good barometer for whether they are giving them enough attention. Our children are only with us for a relatively short time, and making an effort to give each child what they need of us is so much more rewarding than time spent dealing with arguments. It's not always possible, but it's worth bearing in mind.

It's lovely when siblings grow up to be lifelong friends, but it doesn't always work out that way. At the very least we want family life to be pleasant and respectful, and you have a lot of influence over that. It often starts with your own happiness, followed by giving priority to meeting the needs of each family member as best you can.

PARENTING TOOLS FOR FAMILY HARMONY

Family mealtimes and family meetings are parenting tools that can support you throughout your time raising a family. They are particularly important when life is busy or communication has become strained, as often happens in the teenage years.

Mealtimes matter

Some say that family mealtimes seem to be at the root of all that is good and wholesome. Social research in a number of areas (happiness, academic success, drinking, drugs, teenage pregnancy) shows that family meals are crucial – sometimes even more than social class, financial or family situation.[4] Family meals aren't always harmonious: someone may not like what is being served, the chat may be combative, the meal rushed

4 K.R. Lora et al., 'Frequency of family meals and 6–11-year-old children's social behaviors', *Journal of Family Psychology*, 28 (2014), 577–582.

– and at least one person at the table may rather be somewhere else. But it appears that even family digestion laced with tension is better than individuals grabbing a bite on the run or eating alone in front of a screen. So if family meals are a key to future happiness, I'm jolly well going to have them! Mealtimes were sacred in my childhood home and I hated it. Mind you, hating it doesn't necessarily mean that I didn't benefit from it.

How can we make family meals more enjoyable?

- When everyone's home, make those meals special, and worry less about grabbing food on days when schedules don't coincide.
- Simpler meals that take less time to cook leave more time for eating together.
- When we're not in a rush, we're all more pleasant – and so is the meal.
- Involve family in food preparation: if they had a hand in making it they will enjoy it more.
- Make meals that can be adjusted for different tastes.
- Ban name-calling, teasing, interrupting, leaving the table early and mobiles.
- Don't use the opportunity to tackle that hot family issue where everyone is bound to disagree.
- Make an effort, just as you would if you invited friends over.

'Brown rice is not food!'

Everyone else's home is apparently a smorgasbord of appetising treats, while ours is declared a boring-food zone. My teenager is going through a growth spurt and she wants to fuel it with chocolate and ice cream. Then I have to remember that I lived on iced coffee and peanuts in my late teens and I survived – even evolved into a wholefood mum. I have to trust that my child's taste buds and body know enough about nutritious eating from the first decade or so that she will return there once forays into the land of Pot Noodles and Chewits have been made. So we prioritise family harmony over perfect eating, accommodating changing tastes in exchange for a continued willingness to all sit down together.

Family meetings

Some family arguments cycle round and never seem to get resolved. The same things are fought over, the same accusations hurled, nobody feels heard, and nothing changes. Family meetings can help parents and children to pull together and understand each other better. When everyone has a chance to speak and each opinion is respected, stuck patterns can be resolved and compromise found. Family meetings can be informal, called by any member of the family, last only twenty minutes and create a culture of working together to deal with problems.

Arlene calls a family meeting to curb the constant fighting with her daughter

Tensions in our house were building. My teenager didn't want me telling her what to do – but then she wasn't doing what she needed to. The more stressed I became over late nights, rushed departures and forgotten homework, the more she dug her heels in. Each of us felt that our life was being blighted by the other. Time for a family meeting! First her dad and I discussed a fair approach. Then we found a time we could sit down with our teen, when no one had to dash off anywhere and the younger children were elsewhere. We started with each of us saying the one thing we most wanted to change. As we talked we were always conscious that we were two adults facing one child and how that might feel for her. We ended up with a short list of proposed compromises to try for a week. The atmosphere in the house lifted; even though many of the niggles carried on, they gradually waned and our feelings towards one another improved immeasurably.

CHAPTER SIX

Managing her wild and magnificent moods

Okay, buckle up – the ride's getting bumpy. Your teen's emotions are going to reverberate through your family, rattle the house and take you to your limits. Gabrielle Roth, one of my mentors, used to say that emotions are energy in motion. The ride that your teen is on is an exciting one, and the shake-up can benefit the whole family.

In this chapter, I describe some of the changes happening in a teenager's brain. This should help us to understand more about her behaviour and her needs.

As the intensity of your teen's emotions changes, she needs to learn to manage them and avoid numbing out. You are required to set her a good example, to be present and in touch with her to ensure that she is well and that coping strategies such as drinking, eating disorders, self-harm or even suicide attempts don't creep in unannounced. It is also important that essential influences on her mood, such as lack of sleep or exam pressure, are handled well. At the end of the chapter, I provide a number of ways in which you can keep your connection strong through this time of change and challenge.

A TEEN'S BRAIN IS SPECIAL

'What were you thinking?' Crazy, irrational, impulsive behaviour – what possesses our teens to act this way?

We often judge our teens for being moody, reckless, directionless, obsessed with their image and their peers. Instead, we could be complimenting them for being perfectly poised during this transitional stage in their lives. A teenage brain is in a state of flux, which recent research indicates is well suited to the teen's task of forging ahead into adult life.[1]

Teenage brains go through a crazy phase. They don't think like us, or how they did when they were younger. Teeming with hormones, the teenage brain is under major reconstruction, with earlier connections in the brain being broken and new ones forming. The prefrontal cortex, the centre of reasoning and impulse control, is very much a work in progress, making adolescence a time of roller-coaster emotions and 'interesting' judgements.

Imaging research on the teenage brain by the National Institute of Mental Health studied over a hundred young people as they grew up in the 1990s.[2] Between the ages of twelve and twenty-five major reorganisation takes place, resulting in a faster and more sophisticated brain. The brain's axons – nerve fibres that send signals between neurons – are gradually coated in myelin, boosting transmission speed by up to a hundred times. The dendrites – branchlike extensions that neurons use to receive signals from nearby axons – grow twiggier, the most-used synapses grow stronger and the less-used ones wither.

A teenager's brain can work clumsily during these changes, as she awkwardly masters its increased speed and specialisation. We often view the resultant impulsive, sensation-seeking, risk-taking, peer-orientated behaviour as a design fault, but actually this phase is highly flexible and adaptable, perfect for the job that teens face of establishing themselves out in the world.

1 Nicola Morgan, *Blame My Brain: The Amazing Teenage Brain Revealed* (Walker, 2013).
2 Jay Giedd, 'Structural magnetic resonance imaging of the adolescent brain', *Annals of the New York Academy of Sciences*, 1021 (2004), 77–85.

This openness to experimenting is hugely beneficial as teens venture forth from the relative safety of home into less-known terrains, carving out their future. Sensation-seeking can be dangerous, but it also leads to meeting new people and going to new places. Focusing heavily on spending time with peers can help build essential social skills. A pull towards novelty can lead directly to useful new experience. A willingness to take risks can confer an advantage.

If it doesn't damage or kill them, it will strengthen them!

Teens learn things differently. When our children are little they learn by copying. They mimic what they see and hear, and practise in play what they witness. As they approach adolescence they enter a time of self-discovery and need to try things their own way. This breaking away is essential for the healthy development of a young adult, but it often proves tricky for parents. It's not rebellion. It's nature's way, and it helps our young people on their journey of discovering themselves.

Let your teen know that you are behind her – even when she doesn't seem to know what she is doing or why and neither do you!

What a teen learns at this stage carries more weight as once their brain's wiring is upgraded the connections are harder to change.

Teens feel things differently. While the areas for logic and strategic planning are under reconstruction, the emotional centres are active and unrestrained. These changes in the brain make it a time of heightened emotional sensitivity – their feelings are bigger and wilder – and teens naturally have less emotional control. At the same time, they are relatively new to taking responsibility for their emotional wellbeing and don't always know how to cope. Small triggers can signal the end of the world to them – and that's normal. When the skirt your daughter was planning to wear today is found to be dirty, it might really mean that she cannot face the day. When you give a curfew, it can seem to threaten to ruin her life! When relationships fail, it really can feel like all future happiness is doomed.

Although a teen's emotions can seem ridiculously out of proportion and her actions inexplicable, we need to give her our loving support rather than our judgement. If we belittle her feelings or don't take her actions seriously, we risk extreme reactions. Nobody likes to be trivialised, least of all a teenager. She needs help with her tendency to over-express her feelings, or to bury them, and we need to learn not to take her outbursts personally. Your teen needs the diplomatic guidance of the adults around her. She needs you to validate her experience while not getting caught up in the drama; and sometimes she needs you to do her thinking for her, helping her to plan what she will do if she misses the bus and how to remember her sports kit on Fridays.

When a biddable daughter transforms into a truculent teen, it is easy for parents to focus on the negative aspects and forget that, even though their teen is behaving as if she doesn't care, she does care – and deeply. We have a cultural tendency to talk about teens as if they have no feelings. When she acts tough, we can forget that she is at one of the most sensitive stages of her life. This is why adults in communities in olden times became very involved in a young person's life at adolescence, taking on the task of mentoring them, disciplining them and coaching them in readiness for adult life ahead. Our teens have a growing desire for freedom, but they need guidance in taking the extra responsibility that goes with that. They want space from their parents, but they need other adults to help them with the scary prospect of making it out in the world. Their peers are vital allies, on the same path but too caught up in their own journey to be the wisest guides. The best thing you can do is give your child an environment that feels loving, accepting and safe. Find her some mentors and, better still, an adult-led youth group or a Girls Journeying Together group.

The teenage years are a crucial period of learning, and what teens learn at this time has a powerful impact on their future. We can support this transition by being engaged, guiding our teens with a light but steady hand, staying connected but allowing independence. And helping them to realise the importance of getting enough sleep!

Corinne is desperate to fit in

Corinne wanted a new school bag. She already had a perfectly good one, but it wasn't like everyone else's. Her dad told her to get one online, but when she asked her mum for credit card details her mum questioned her need for another bag. 'But mine's not the right kind,' Corinne implored her. Then she began her campaign of whining, and when that didn't work she burst into tears, 'You don't understand! I need a new bag. I can't go to school with this one.' On Monday came the shock: 'I hate you, I hate you. I'm not going to school. You can't make me.' What her parents didn't know was that Corinne had been teased about her bag and she didn't feel secure enough in herself or in her friendship group to think that the solution could be anything other than a new bag.

TEENAGE GIRLS LOVE TO HATE THEIR MOTHERS

Mothers often get the worst of their daughter's behaviour. How is it that her friends' mothers say she is lovely to have around – considerate, polite, friendly – but the minute she closes your front door your daughter turns into someone else entirely?

The ups and downs of a teenage girl's life are hard for her to handle. She is still learning how to manage strong feelings, and her hormonal swings can take her on an emotional roller coaster. Her best friends can seem like a lifeline to her. They know what she is going through because they are going through it too: she's not alone. But it's often with Mum that she acts out her frustrations and tensions. Lucky you!

When life's pressures overwhelm her, your daughter lets off steam where she feels safest – with you, trusting that you are going to keep on loving her. You are not going to give her detention, put her down or shun her from the group. You are going to keep on being there for her, caring about her, even when she behaves like she doesn't deserve it. Children don't have to earn their parents' love.

Sometimes our teens need us to make allowances, as they aren't entirely in charge of their behaviour while their hormones rage and their brains reconfigure. They need clear boundaries about what is not acceptable, and loving forgiveness when they slip up. Teens tantrum, and we need to cast our minds back to what worked with toddler tantrums: listening, not shouting, loving firmness. That doesn't mean we tolerate and condone poor behaviour; but by understanding it we can deal with it better.

Set clear limits. Get support from other parents of teens, drawing on the reassurance and wisdom of experience. Have somewhere away from your teen that you can let off steam too. You may not have the pleasure of experiencing the lovely version of your daughter that your friends report, but be the grown-up and don't take it personally.

. . . .

Living with a teenager is a challenge, but so is being one.

As the parent, you need to be the one who takes charge of the situation with loving compassion.

. . . .

Time for the grown-ups to grow up

It's natural for our teenagers to trigger our extreme emotions. They want us to feel how they feel, and they know how to do it: they've had a lifetime to study us, and in many ways they are like us. They can bring out the worst in us, and we hate it. It is so easy to blame them for how we feel, and so much more challenging to look into the mirror they are holding up to us: sometimes we don't manage our emotions well – we lose it, seeking to control, blame and punish in order to try to get our own way. This is not the time for a screaming match, guilting her with criticism or giving her the angry silent treatment. Your teenager needs you to be the adult so she can learn how to be one.

. . . .

Take on the teenager's challenge – grow up!

. . . .

If the child in you is surfacing and shouting to be heard, find a trusted friend to talk to or sign up for a few counselling sessions so that you can attend to the part of you that still needs to be listened to. Dig deep and do whatever it takes to bring out the best in yourself in your dealings with your teenager. Then take time out, alone or in the supportive company of other adults, to replenish and resource yourself, especially when you find yourself slipping back into your own childish ways.

. . . .

Give what you want and in time you will get back what you gave.

. . . .

Losing my cool

I had a fight with my teen this morning. I forgot to put the health of our relationship first and reached for whatever I could say to make her do what I thought was best. So I lost my authority. She stormed out and I worried about her all day. And fumed. And felt irritated that I'd lost my cool.

I forgot that being her mother gives me influence – but only if I can conduct myself respectfully. Instead I felt powerless, like a child, and we fought like two children desperately trying to assert ourselves.

The way I spoke, my teen was unable to listen to me.

The way I tried to enforce my point of view, my teen was unable to heed me.

In the end she did what she wanted to do: cycle into the village on a dangerous country lane to catch her bus, with her helmet on but no lights or bike lock, and no plan for how she would get home after dark. She survived! She got home safely – and tomorrow we'll discover if her bike is still where she left it!

Don't make your daughter wrong

Do you wish that your daughter were different? Don't, because that makes her wrong.

Do you believe that you can tell your child how to change and then she will? Don't – it's not respectful and it doesn't work.

. . . .

Love someone exactly as they are and
watch them transform into the best version of themselves.

. . . .

My parenting changed when I stopped seeing my child's challenging behaviour as 'bad'. Instead I asked myself, 'What problem is she trying to solve by behaving like this?' For example, a teenager is banging about the house: she is bored, she doesn't want help with the homework that she's stuck on, apparently there's never anything decent to eat in the house, and it's all your fault because you live in the country miles from friends. You can feel your anger rising at the way that she talks to you, and how she dampens the atmosphere of wherever she slumps herself. However, if you pause and look at her, you can see that she is unhappy. Really unhappy. Sure, the way she is communicating her unhappiness is not pleasant, but if you can refrain from reacting to that and respond to her sadness instead, you can actually help her.

Teenagers aren't always easy to reach, but everyone, no matter what their age, feels better for knowing that someone cares enough to notice. Finding the right words and the right tone helps. 'You're stuck on your homework, and you wish we lived in the town. I can see you're not at all happy.' And next time you behave in a way you regret, try asking yourself, 'What problem was I trying to solve? How could I have solved it differently?'

. . . .

Bad behaviour is an attempt to solve a problem.

. . . .

MANAGING MOODS

Okay, so the first thing to check out is how you are at managing your own moods. Children of all ages often take their lead from us, so if you are one for losing your temper and shouting, sulking or saying mean things, then you will have to sort your own act out before you can expect your daughter to. We all behave badly from time to time – that's normal, and we need to forgive ourselves. It's just that if you haven't learned to deal with your own strong feelings it will be hard to show your daughter how to do it.

Let her know how you cope when you are sad, angry or frightened. Experiment with her to find out what works for her. If you are not sure what to try, suggest creativity, movement, talking or relaxing. Some children find it helpful to tell someone about how they are feeling, though they might need help to identify the 'right' someone who can listen and not judge. Sometimes the best thing for dealing with strong feelings is to get active to release the tension, dance to loud music, run, go swimming. Many children already have a host of ways to soothe themselves: stroking a pet, reading, baking, listening to music. Otherwise, turn it into art. Help your daughter find ways of being creative: writing in a diary, painting, making things, cooking. If you have done these things with your daughter throughout her childhood it will become her natural response to turn to them as outlets when she is troubled.

. . . .

In a nutshell, sort your own moods first, and then help her to talk, create, move or self-soothe to manage hers.

. . . .

Many teens run into difficulties and need help. Your child needs you to take her seriously and to be able to guide her through the storms of her emotions; you need to find a way not to take her moods personally. You must be able to hold onto the bigger picture for her. She needs you to have a sense of perspective while she can't, without making light of what she is going through. At the same time, if your instincts tell you that something is deeply wrong, avoid the temptation to put it down to her 'being a teen'. How to guide your daughter away from self-harm and out of depression is tackled in Chapter Seven.

Things to remember when your daughter is angry

An angry teen is a vulnerable teen. Feeling angry is not comfortable – it can feel scary and out of control.

There is no single right way to deal with an angry teen, but there are many wrong ways – and you are likely to try some of them! Your daughter will let you know when you get it wrong, but she may not let you know when you get it right.

Teens have lots of good reasons to feel angry, and their anger often hides feelings that are harder to show, like fear, hurt, loneliness or despair. A teen's anger needs to be met with compassion. Angry teens push away when they often need you to stay. An angry teen is less angry once her anger is acknowledged, and she may manage her anger better if she can be helped to notice what triggers it.

Anger needs safe expression. You will be frightened of your teen's anger if you are frightened of your own. You may need to set boundaries about how it is expressed (such as no violence towards herself or another person). Back a teen into a corner, and you will enrage or cower her. Saving face is hugely important to a teen.

Anger can provide energy for a positive change. Anger can be released by getting active and doing something physical or by using it to fuel creative expression such as writing, drawing or singing. Playing angry music can offer a great release. Comedy can give an angry teen a break. Find support – don't try to manage an angry teen alone.

Teens' everyday grief

We don't usually think of teenagers as being full of grief and sadness, but they can be, and they often don't have the resources to deal with it. There's the everyday grief of your teen's childhood passing, her body changing and friendships fluctuating. Then there are the deeper losses such as parents separating, grandparents or pets dying, moving house, a romance ending, and other life shocks. It's hard to witness grief in our child or know how to help her through it if we have not learnt how to grieve healthily ourselves.

Adolescence can be stressful as well as exciting. While enjoying more adult freedoms, some childhood pleasures are lost and mourned for. Children can be resistant to change, as they don't have the life experience to know that they will survive it and, better still, may even benefit from it. Teens experience loss more acutely because their brains are different. Not being invited to a party or being let down by a friend can really be traumatic. Many of us adults forget the heightened feelings of our teenage years, so we sometimes lack compassion.

In Girls Journeying Together we examine the events that have had the most impact on each girl's life – divorce and the death of grandparents and pets feature large. Everyone deals with loss differently, but I often hear girls talk of hiding their grief and feeling isolated: 'I don't want to upset my mum.' 'Dad has enough to worry about at the moment.' 'They wouldn't understand anyway – it probably just seems silly to them.'

When a teen doesn't feel able to cope with her feelings, disordered eating, drinking and cutting are some of the unhealthy ways that she may resort to when overwhelmed. It is important to be alert to our teens' grief and give it credence, no matter how insignificant the trigger may seem to us. Your teen needs your nurturing care even when she doesn't know how to ask for it and her behaviour pushes you away – especially then.

Lulu cuts herself when it all gets too much

Lulu was upset – again. This time it was over a maths test tomorrow that she felt sure she was going to fail. She was in her room studying and she shouted at her mum when she came up to tell her that dinner was ready. Her mum started by trying to reassure her that she'd do okay, that she must spare time to eat, but Lulu carried on being rude, and her mum lost her temper. Unable to bear the added stress of her mum shouting, Lulu locked herself in the bathroom. She took a knife she had hidden there, ran it across her arm, and a sense of calm descended on her. All the anxiety about the test and the guilt about shouting at her mum dissolved as she watched the blood trickle down her arm.

But feeling calm didn't last, the anxiety came back and Lulu felt compelled to cut herself again.

Is your daughter being bullied?

Many children who are bullied tell no one. A bullied child often feels shame and believes that she is to blame for being bullied – so her impulse is to hide it. Teens are even more likely to take bullying as a sign of their own personal weakness. They won't want others to know, and they believe they should be able to handle it themselves. Many parents believe that their child will come to them if they run into difficulties, perhaps unaware of how hard it may be to speak out.

Bullying is horrible. It makes you want to die. But you can't tell, you just can't. If you think you know someone is being bullied, don't pretend it's not happening, even if they tell you that nothing's wrong. If you think there is, then do something.

Amber (age thirteen)

Girls on the spectrum

Autism Spectrum Disorder is often not suspected in girls until they run into difficulties in their teens. Even then it can remain misdiagnosed or undiagnosed, especially in bright girls who have learnt to cover up their social awkwardness. Girls on the spectrum are more likely to be bullied, withdraw and become depressed, or suffer anxiety, obsessive behaviour, sleep problems or eating disorders. When the focus shifts to understanding how to manage their social challenges, everything else improves.

Numbing out – hoping the feelings will go away

You do it, I do it, our teenagers do it – it's commonplace. Checking Facebook, online messaging, watching television, listening to music, reading, eating, gaming, talking on the phone, texting, drinking, smoking,

drug taking, extreme sports, exercising, working, tidying, sleeping…
Not necessarily all avoidance activities, but they can be. No matter how
well things may be going at school or with your daughter's friends and
hobbies, the teenage years are unsettling. It's natural for life to overwhelm
her at times and for her to try to dampen the feelings of anxiety, anger,
sadness, fear or even exuberance. It's understandable that she seeks the
undemanding familiarity of the television show, computer game or food
cupboard.

There's nothing wrong with reaching for comfort when all seems too
much. It's only a concern if someone, child or adult, repeatedly looks
for comfort in the wrong places. No long-term relief is found in alcohol,
a bowl of ice cream or yet another evening spent on the computer. No
real resolution is gained by staying in bed, constant social networking
or smoking. Sadly, some ways of coping are addictive, and often the
problems that lie beneath are never addressed.

Yelling at our teenagers to leave the screen, curb their drinking or get out
of bed is not going to help them deal with their feelings. If you hassle your
teen to change her behaviour, you turn it into a battle with you instead of
the one she is having with herself. At some level she knows when she is
using something as an escape, and deep down she will sense that this isn't
serving her. You do your daughter a major disservice if you focus on her
not-done homework, her eating or her downtime activities instead
of considering what is going on inside her that is making her want to
'numb out'.

The challenge of living with a teenager is learning how to embrace
the force of her feelings and be unfazed. Not to try to fix things, but to
trust that this is part of her journey and help her through. We want our
daughters to dare to experience the range and strength of their emotions.
We want them to be in touch with their feelings but not to get stuck,
learning ways to manage their irritability, rage, envy, insecurity, sorrow,
love, excitement, despair and disorientation. We want them to reach
out to friends or family for the support that they need. Strong feelings,

especially if aimed at us, can be uncomfortable, but it's important not to squash them or diminish them. Let your daughter vent, weep or worry; listen to her, sympathise and wait. Rather than pressuring her to tell you how to help, which she quite probably can't do, ponder aloud, 'I wonder what would be of help here?' and wait; even if she doesn't have any ideas it will get her wondering. If you can tolerate your teenager's feelings, it communicates to her that she will be able to handle them too.

Teen drinking

We each have to decide our parenting approach to drinking. Alcohol is clearly an adult activity and teens press for access to the adult domain. At what age would you pour your child a drink? What do you do when you know that alcohol will be at a teen party? How about when you suspect that your under-age teenager is meeting mates in the pub?

We want them to find their safe level without coming to any harm in the process.

Alcohol is an adult pleasure, used to celebrate and socialise – so how magical this grown-ups' elixir must seem! No wonder it must appear to be one of the keys to the gateway to adulthood.

Children believe that part of being an adult is to drink, yet a child's liver is less well equipped to cope with alcohol, and her brain is less able to manage moderation. Vulnerable to peer pressure, there is a teen culture of egging each other on – teenagers take risks in groups that they would not take individually: over-drinking, larking about, damaging property, climbing, stealing, fighting, sexual activity, driving dangerously.

We have laws about alcohol. In England you must be eighteen years old to purchase alcohol but you can drink it with your parents at home from the age of five. A sixteen-year-old can drink (but not buy) alcohol in a pub if with an adult and the drink is with a meal. You may not drive if you have had more than a certain amount to drink. We hand a teenager a cider about the same time as we hand her the car keys, and this has the potential to be a lethal combination. And while we insist on driving lessons and a test before a person is free to drive alone, no such training or test is given with alcohol consumption.

Just as our youngsters become especially self-conscious socially, we sanction the use of something that alleviates some of that awkwardness – and then we leave them to it. We ask too much of our teenagers when we leave them unsupervised with alcohol. They misbehave, they injure themselves, they become pregnant – often invoking the excuse of drunkenness. And we let it happen.

We are so anxious not to intrude in their social lives that we abandon them to danger. More than half of all first sexual experiences happen when drunk, and more often than not the sex is unprotected. Many young people live to regret the fights, criminal damage, accidents, injury and pregnancy arising from uncontrolled drinking, but not all survive. I would not wish for my daughter's first sexual encounter to be experienced drunk. Let them resent our discreet presence at their parties, in their youth clubs, wherever they hang out. Be willing to give your life over in the same way now as you did when your daughter was a toddler. Teens need us to be there just as vigilantly. We have the right to supervise and work out how to be involved as care-takers.

Research shows that underage drinking is reduced when parents talk regularly to their children about drinking.[3] Mothers Against Drunk Driving has collated the information from this research into an online guide for parents.[4] Whether you favour abstinence or learning by experimentation, make sure your teen knows:

How much alcohol is too much alcohol. Line up a range of drinks (or find a website that can do this for you) to demonstrate how many units of

---

3 Renske Spijkerman, Regina J. J. M. van den Eijnden & Annemarie Huiberts, 'Socioeconomic differences in alcohol-specific parenting practices and adolescents' drinking patterns', *European Addiction Research*, 14(1) (2008), 26–37.

4 https://www.madd.org/the-solution/power-of-parents/

alcohol are in different drinks. Wines can vary enormously in alcoholic content; beers too. Spirits cannot be drunk in the same volume as other drinks. Discuss how much alcohol a body can safely handle.

How to stay safe. Make sure your teen knows to:

- Eat before and while drinking.
- Start the evening with something to quench thirst.
- Alternate every drink with a glass of water.
- Finish the evening with a pint of water.

Impress on your teen the importance of looking out for each other if drinking:

- Know to put anyone who falls asleep while drunk into the recovery position. (Death by choking on vomit is all too common.)
- Nominate a 'drinking safe-person' who will not drink and will look out for others in the group.

Finally, if your teen is regularly getting drunk, pause to consider why . . .

Lack of sleep making everything worse

Did you know that teens need an hour or two more sleep than adults[5] but often get less? And that they become night owls for a while, not feeling drowsy until later and needing to sleep in longer in the mornings? And that over three-quarters of teens are sleep-deprived?[6]

Statistics show that teens who don't get sufficient sleep are more prone to suicidal feelings, and more likely to smoke, drink, use drugs or zone out on

---

5   Ann Hagell, 'Adolescent sleep', AYPH Research Update No.10 (July 2012). http://www. youngpeopleshealth.org.uk/wp-content/uploads/2015/07/Sleep.pdf
6   Ruthann Richter, 'Among teens, sleep deprivation an epidemic', Stanford University School of Medicine (October 2015). https://med.stanford.edu/news/all-news/2015/10/among-teens-sleep-deprivation-an-epidemic.html

the computer.[7] So, if you are worried about any of these things, make sure your teen gets enough sleep – possibly a simple and effective solution to a complex problem.

In addition to the fact that teens love a lie-in but loathe an early night, time for sleep is being squeezed out because:

- Teens need eight to ten hours' sleep a night, but many don't feel like going to bed much before midnight because their circadian rhythms temporarily change, with a later release of the 'darkness hormone' melatonin, and most have to get up for school less than seven hours later.
- At the same time their lives are filling up with extra studying, hobbies, socialising and social media.
- Many parents are more relaxed about having screens in a teenager's bedroom and let the teen choose when to go to sleep.

All this is leading to chronic sleep deprivation in our teens. And lack of sleep slows down the body's systems, leading to:

- Poor performance academically, physically and emotionally.
- Difficulty concentrating and remembering.
- Being slower and less able in sport.
- Loss of motivation.
- Slower healing and more susceptibility to illness and injury.
- Poor skin, acne, pallor.
- Food cravings, poor diet choices, nocturnal eating and weight gain.
- Sadness, hopelessness and depression.
- Moodiness, irritability, aggression, impulsivity.
- Feelings of anxiety and stress – which can, in turn, hinder sleep.

7   Sakari Lemola et al., 'Adolescents' electronic media use at night, sleep disturbance, and depressive symptoms in the smartphone age', *Journal of Youth and Adolescence*, 44(2) (2015), 405–18.

Do you recognise these symptoms of lack of sleep as being those characteristics commonly ascribed to teens?

. . . .

It is possible teens are not innately moody and unmotivated, but are suffering from insufficient sleep.

. . . .

Sleep is brain food. Teens need sleep to support the growth spurt and sexual maturation that are occurring; a hormone essential to both is released during sleep. At a time when increased demands are being made academically, teens need to be alert and able to function well. Adolescence is a time of huge shifts in self-awareness, socially and emotionally, and teens need not be hampered by poor mood. Experiments with a later school start time for teenagers have resulted in much improved performance and behaviour.

Parents are essential in assisting in their teens' sleep. Older children can settle themselves, but many appreciate our company at bedtime just as they did when they were little. Teens often come to life in the evening. If you are available, you may find that your teen chooses bedtime for talking about her day and spilling out her worries. This might not happen at any other time. It will strengthen your relationship if you are willing to interrupt your own evening to join her for a while at the end of her day.

Badgering a teen to go to bed doesn't work! Instead, our growing children need to understand for themselves the advantages of settling to bed in good time and having enough sleep. Establishing good sleep habits is a lifetime gift to your child.

Aids to a good night's sleep:

- Set a regular bedtime and wake-up time to get the body into the habit of getting enough sleep.
- Take regular exercise, but not just before bed.

- Have a bedtime routine of restful activity: a book, music, bath, low lights – avoid screens and snacking.
- Make the bedroom a cool, dark, sleep haven.
- Read to your daughter, sit on the edge of the bed to chat in the dark, potter about on the landing.
- Teach your daughter how to use her mind and her breath to relax her body with relaxation techniques.
- Model good bedtime behaviour yourself.

* *

It might be this simple: a good night's sleep, night after night, may be the answer to many of the problems experienced by teens and their parents!

* *

Coping well with exam stress

Charities for children's wellbeing are reporting that exams are an increasing source of stress and mental health issues.[8] The trouble for parents who want to support their child safely through her exams is that a lot of the best tips for managing exam stress sound incredibly like the nagging we may have been doing for years: eat healthily, go to bed early, exercise, plan ahead, read the questions carefully, check your answers, don't worry. Easier said than done (especially that last one), as we know from our own experience – or we'd all be well slept, exercised, fed, organised, stimulated, productive and relaxed!

Take some of the pressure off your teen. During exams, make her life easier wherever you can and whenever she will let you. You may feel that your teen is old enough to take responsibility for her own sleep, washing, eating, planning, exercise, time management and motivation – and perhaps normally she is, but exam-time isn't 'normal' time. Remember

8 'Exam stress overwhelming for thousands of children', NSPCC News (12 May 2017). https://www.nspcc.org.uk/what-we-do/news-opinion/exam-stress-overwhelming-for-thousands-of-children/

how much better you can cope in times of high demand when someone else shoulders some of your responsibilities.

Websites offering good advice to teens about how to cope with exams are plentiful, but this may not be an easy time for your teen to take in advice or put it into action. So *you* do it. Read the advice and trust your instincts about which information will be most relevant to your child. Then get creative in assisting her to improve her exam coping skills.

Here are some examples (but you will need to tailor-make yours to suit your own circumstances):

- **Better sleep** – buy her some Epsom salts or lavender oil to add to a relaxing bath that you run half an hour before a sensible bedtime.
- **Improved diet** – rather than fretting about her eating junk, fill her plate and your cupboards with healthy, appetising treats (peaches, dried mango, cashew nuts, hot chocolate to replace coffee), cook her favourite dishes, boil her an egg for breakfast.
- **Motivation** – especially if your child is having trouble motivating herself, know that your nudging or nagging will get her down. Make it your job to acknowledge when she does manage to study; give thought to what gets in the way when she doesn't manage to study, and to how you could help.
- **Laundry** – do hers: gather in the dirties, wash, dry, sort and put them away. One less thing for her to do.
- **Water** – fill her water bottle for the day and place a glass of water with a slice of lemon on her desk while she studies.
- **Exercise and breaks** – offer to go swimming, walk the dog with her, or take her and her friends dancing.
- **Perspective** – be aware of how you talk about exams, and don't make them sound as if they are everything. Childline reports that young people feel that parents are often the source of unbearable exam pressure. Be around to listen after an exam; don't dwell on mistakes, but focus on what still lies ahead, and suggest your daughter avoids anxious or competitive talk with friends.

- **Take slow, deep breaths** when you are stressed – let her see how that helps you to collect yourself.
- **Self-talk** – make yours audible: 'This is hard, but I'm not beaten yet.'

Do more for your child during exam-time so that, leading by example, you show her how to take care of herself when she is feeling stressed. Once the exams are over, she can take responsibility again. She might not appreciate you just now, so hold on to the knowledge that the majority of young women in their mid-twenties are full of praise for how much their mothers did for them in their difficult adolescent years.

Finally, if you are getting stressed about your daughter's exams, take heed of the checklist yourself on how to manage exam stress!

. . . .

How we help our children to manage exam stress – or any
stress – gives them tools for life.

. . . .

KEEPING A STRONG CONNECTION WITH HER

As they head towards their teens many girls are scared by how easily they are moved to tears or into a wild fury or a panic. If your daughter can express her feelings in some way to someone, they immediately become more manageable. There are many ways to do this – not just talking. But talking is good.

Parents often ask me how to talk with a teenager who doesn't seem to want to. Generally, girls are desperate to talk but not always to someone as close as a parent. Find her an 'auntie' or two, key women in her life she can depend on, and don't be offended if she doesn't turn to you first.

You also want to be the kind of listener that your daughter feels like talking to. Many parents find it hard to hear their child when she is distressed, and it's natural for us to want to make it better, but teens tell me that they hate it when we try to fix things. They just want us to listen while they get it all out. They want us to keep listening while they figure a way through. If you can sit beside your daughter while she expresses whatever is going on inside, without judging, minimising or rescuing, it gives her a sense of her feelings being important, valid and manageable.

A child's choice of her best time to talk is often not yours – but make the most of the opportunity, as you may not get it again. Teens often favour the car, the dark at bedtime, when they are ill, or when you are busy and distracted!

Maisie confides in her dad

Maisie's dad was bringing her up on his own. He had dealt with the approach of puberty by asking his sister to have a few womanly chats with her. Maisie was close to her dad, but in her mid-teens she became withdrawn. No amount of gentle questioning could draw her out, so her dad decided to take Maisie and her friends to an amusement park to see if this would break down barriers. They had a great day, ate too much ice cream and managed not to puke on the rides. On the journey home the teens were all in high spirits, chattering away in the back of the car. Maisie's dad listened quietly as their conversation turned to why Maisie's best friend Carrie hadn't come with them – it turned out that her boyfriend didn't like her going anywhere without him.

That night Maisie's dad sat on the side of Maisie's bed and wondered aloud whether she missed Carrie, and Maisie began to open up. She felt like she'd lost her best friend, but she was also worried for Carrie. Carrie's boyfriend was pressurising her to do all sorts of things that Maisie didn't think were right – but, worse than that, Carrie was starving herself and hiding it. Carrie had made Maisie promise not to tell anyone, and now Maisie felt lonely and sick with worry. After the relief of telling her dad, their relationship returned to its old closeness and he helped her speak to Carrie so that Carrie eventually asked for some adult help.

When my daughter was little she used to chatter on and on with all manner of important things to tell me, at great length. I'd listen, but I also had meals to cook, and work to do, and other children to attend to, and, and, and ... Then one day when she was in full flow I caught myself making a shopping list in my head. I stopped. I knelt down so that I could be on her level and I asked her to start again. She smiled and let out a huge sigh – she finally had my undivided attention.

. . . .

Listen to your little one so that she will carry on telling you stuff when she's big.

. . . .

Mothers of teens often complain that their daughters no longer talk to them. If your daughter isn't a teen yet then listen to her when she is little, even when what she is telling you seems inconsequential or dull. Don't stop listening, and then she's less likely to stop telling you things as she grows older. And when she is older, listen to her even when what she is saying seems trivial. How you listen when she is telling you the mundane things will determine how willing she is to tell you about more sensitive things. Mothers who make regular time for Mother–Daughter Dates report that communication becomes freer as a result.

I remember how my daughter would come to me for a hug and would reproach me with, 'No, a full-attention cuddle!' and I knew to drop everything, including the chatter inside my head, and give her all of me. Children know. They know if you are really paying attention. And they know if you are listening supportively or critically. So, if you really want your daughter to talk to you when she is a teen, pay really good attention to whatever she has to say to you.

Opening doors to your teen's heart

The teen years can be a time of increased privacy, misunderstandings and children turning to friends more than to their parents. It takes sensitivity to reach your teen, mend bridges and stay in touch with what is important to her. Make the most of times when communication is easier: when she arrives home, at bedtime or when sick, in the car or through films.

Homecoming welcome

I'm sometimes greeted with a hug and a torrent of information when my child arrives home; other times she seems a bit distant and reluctant to answer my questions. I want to respect her space, but it's also important to reconnect after time apart, as otherwise that feeling of detachment can drift into the remainder of the day.

For some children, stepping over the threshold of home allows all the feelings that have been contained during the day to well up. When a welcoming parent is met by a grumpy, glum or uptight child, it can be tempting to reproach or probe. Experiment with pausing for a minute when your daughter arrives home, showing her that you are happy to see her and offering something: a drink, a cuddle, a shoulder massage. Some people need five minutes alone on returning home. If this is so for your daughter, give her that, but then seek her out.

* *

Make home somewhere she is safe to be herself.

* *

The bedtime gateway

'All I can get out of my daughter these days is that she's "fine" and "nothing really happened" during her day.'

'My daughter's not happy, I know she isn't, but either she can't or else she just won't tell me why.'

'I hear more about my daughter's life from when her friend's mother talks about what her daughter tells her.'

. . . .

If you find some of the old avenues for closeness with your daughter are closing to you, don't forget the gateway of bedtime.

. . . .

Even the toughest children soften at bedtime. There's something about removing the day's clothes and make-up and snuggling under a warm duvet that opens them to allowing in a bit of nurturing. Just look at your teenager's bedroom – often a beloved cuddly toy lingers and a few favourite childhood treasures still adorn her shelves, evidence that a part of her still wants comforting and reassurance even when she seems intent on proving to you and the world that she doesn't need you. The concerns that can be pushed away during the day can begin to worry her as the day draws to a close. Vulnerability surfaces more easily at night and sleepiness dissolves some of the barriers to talking about it.

Hang about in the vicinity of her room, sorting laundry or pottering in your bedroom with the door open, giving off waves of availability. Make an excuse to pop into her room to deliver something forgotten from downstairs or to give her a hot water bottle. With no peers to pass comment she can let her guard down, especially if you are being uninvasive and unpatronising. You may find that she may respond better to simple noticing remarks than to questions. 'Nearly the weekend.' 'Grandma called and sent her love.' 'I felt for you walking in the rain today.' Don't end her day with reprimands or reminders. Bite your tongue and save tackling issues for when she is less vulnerable and not winding down for sleep. If you have been misinterpreting one another recently, be patient while you rebuild trust and prove to her that you are not judging her or wanting her to change.

Your bedtime rituals from when she was younger will give you some pointers for how to connect with your teen now. I have yet to meet a teen who doesn't like being read to, if you can pick the right book and can find a way of getting started so that she doesn't feel silly. Rubbing her back, singing, turning her light out for her – these are all things that you may find she enjoys if she can let you. Many children like to hear stories of when they were young, or when you were. Times of illness are also gateways to recovering closeness, so if she likes you to stroke her hair when she is feverish, just keep on doing it each night long after she feels better unless she asks you to stop. The teenage years can be the most physically deprived, as cuddling with parents begins to feel awkward and the caress of romantic relationships may not be a part of life yet.

Once a physical connection has been made, many girls will open up and begin to share what is on their minds. For others it starts with the talking, and that then makes physical contact possible – such as sitting on her bed, resting your hand on hers or lying beside her.

If they are honest, many parents are just relieved when their teens finally peel off to bed, and are grateful for a moment of that luxury we called 'adult time' when children were younger and still went to bed before us. I have found it hard to make that extra effort to be with my teen at bedtime when all I wanted was to relax at the end of the day, but **some of my best teen parenting is done in the semi-dark of a bedroom as a child settles for the night.**

Healing times

Your daughter looks pale and is complaining of a sore throat, or she feels crampy, weepy and just wants to stay home. Do you see this as an opportunity for her to feel your love and learn how to take care of herself well – or do you worry and wish life was not being interrupted? Make the most of the opportunity that ill health brings to have healing time with your daughter.

Giving time for healing and convalescence isn't easy for working parents, or during academically intense times at school, but we communicate a great deal to our children about the importance of their wellbeing in how we approach illness. Children feel needy when they are not well, and it's good if you can be there, soothing and caring. If we can pause when they need us to, then they learn that their good health is important. They feel that *they* are important.

If you are worried about your daughter's self-esteem, caring for her when she is ill is a powerful way of boosting her sense of having worth. Our words speak volumes, but our actions shout out loud and clear. Surrender yourself to the needs of your patient. Be with her. Sickness can be frightening and lonely, so having your company is reassuring. Fetch flannels, soothing drinks, tempting morsels, audio books. Mop her brow and massage her feet. Do not substitute the television for your presence. Stay with her as she recovers if you can: read to her, play board games, sit at the end of her bed and chat. Allow her to regress. Being cared for when ill can heal past hurts. Illness can be a great time to close the distance that sometimes forms in the teenage years. Love is healing.

In our hurry-up and be-strong culture old-fashioned nursing is so easily replaced by painkillers, symptom suppressants and antibiotics. If you want your child to know how to help her own body to heal, show her that restoring good health is supported by sleep, water, good food, fresh air, loving care and plenty of rest. The body is a self-healing device, but to enable it to heal needs you to reduce other pressures, both physical and emotional. Show your child how to do this by taking good care of her physically and by removing as many of her worries as you can. Phone her school and cancel other commitments; find out the best remedies for what ails her, to reassure yourself and your daughter that you are capable of nursing her back to full health, and give her time.

What are your childhood memories of being sick? Both my parents worked, and we were four children, so illness was an inconvenience. My mother prided herself on never having a single day off sick from work, and we had to pass the thermometer test before we were allowed to stay home. Once we were old enough, we were left on our own, with someone popping home at lunchtime to check we weren't dying. Nursing my children when they are ill doesn't come easily to me. I don't have fond memories of being sick, but I know lots of people who do. I've had to learn to welcome it as a precious time. I knew I'd succeeded when, after I had spent weeks nursing all three children through measles in a darkened room, my little girl said, 'This is like Christmas!' with family time, board games, stories and favourite foods. It takes courage to nurse our sick children rather than give them drugs that mask the symptoms so that we can get on with our lives. Sniffles, coughs, aches and fevers are best not suppressed, and recognising that many symptoms are evidence of the body's healing mechanisms at work means it is important to give time for full recuperation. When I had a publisher's deadline just a few weeks away, my daughter broke her foot and was feeling vulnerable. I didn't write anything for a month as I made her my priority. When we give our children our time, we communicate our love.

. . . .

Make sickness a healing time to treasure.

. . . .

Drive time

Ferrying my children from here to there via that other place is not my bliss. However, I do cherish time alone in the car with a single child. A car is intimate, private, and unconfrontational as we both face front. Silences can happen without being awkward, secret fears can more easily be voiced, private passions likewise.

To make drive time special, let your daughter sit in the passenger seat beside you if she is big enough (even if you don't usually allow it). Keep the radio turned down low enough for talking to be easy, and ban the mobile in exchange for your taxi services. Experiment with speaking less than you would usually and not filling the gaps with your words. Listen, listen, listen – and if you feel the urge to make a judgement, don't! Avoid the old battlegrounds unless she raises one. Try not to solve problems; remain supportive, but hold back on your good advice and invite her ideas for a solution. Find questions that begin with how, what, who, where, when. Have a laugh, be light-hearted. Tell her something about yourself that she doesn't know. Make an effort, the same as you might if your good friend was in the car. (Maybe she is.)

Films are an excellent way of reaching teens

Films can be a great catalyst to inspire your daughter to be all that she can be.

If you want to communicate something, find a film and use it as a springboard for talking.

When you can't get a teen to talk, films can be a way in.

TEENS – THEY DRIVE YOU CRAZY!

- Their incessant demands.
- Blatant disregard for time.
- Mess.
- Noise.
- Spontaneity.
- Persistence.
- Loyalty to their friends.
- Intensity.
- Taking some things so seriously.
- Taking other things not at all seriously.
- Eating exactly what they please – lots or not enough.
- Sleeping lots or not enough.
- Not doing things they don't want to do.
- Doing things that are risky.
- Not telling you anything.
- Doing things that you did when you were their age!

But wait: reread the list. Is it so bad? Some of these qualities we would foster, or seek for ourselves. Perhaps we've a lot to learn from our teens.

TAKEAWAY: TEENS – YOU GOTTA LOVE 'EM!

Teens get such bad press, but I think they are terrific. How is it that we accept the noise and the mess and the tantrums of toddlers but complain bitterly about the noise and the mess and the tantrums of teens? We could be more understanding.

- Their brains are reforming and they are less in control of the prefrontal cortex, where good decisions are made, and the amygdala, where emotions are managed.
- They need more sleep but aren't getting it with early school starts.
- They are working out who they are while under immense pressure to perform at school, match up to impossible ideals, and find their place amongst their peers.
- They are becoming more self-conscious just at a time when their bodies erupt in spots, curves and hormone confusion, making them prone to mental health issues.

Teens are so easily misunderstood. Think back to how you felt when you were a teen and what you needed from the adults around you. No matter how tough they may seem, our teens need us to keep seeing who they are deep down.

. . . .

A teen is a person who wants to love and be loved.

. . . .

Let's love them as they step in through the door, as they go to sleep or ail in bed, as we drive them, nourish them; and let's try to grow up ourselves for their sakes. We love them whatever they do, always, for ever, no matter what.

When you are living with a teenager and learning together how to manage her wild and magnificent moods, it's love she needs. It can help to remember what a special stage of life she is in – and how it won't last!

PART III

Building her tribe of support, including her self

CHAPTER SEVEN

Helping her feel good about herself

The teen years are tough – for the teens and for the parents. Many parents dread the moodiness, preference of friends over family, exam stress, and their children pushing for greater independence. It can get worse: disordered eating, cutting, binge drinking, drug taking, precocious sexual activity, stress and mental health issues are all on the increase in our teenage population.

In my experience, preteen girls hold a sense of themselves that is still relatively positive, but I hear a different story when I talk to teen girls. Too many have learnt to hate themselves: they dislike their bodies, they focus on what they perceive to be their weaknesses, they don't seem to know their own best qualities and they rarely feel good enough. They have lost the trust they once had in their friendships, and their feelings for their parents are ambivalent. Teens' low self-opinion is profoundly affecting their futures. When I listen to teen girls talking about their lives and what they decide to venture into, I see that they are often seriously held back by their lack of confidence. This is why Girls Journeying Together begins when girls are young: to strengthen them against what is to come.

One in three young women in Britain experience suicidal thoughts and one in four have self-harmed;[1] almost one in four fourteen-year-old

---

1 https://www.princes-trust.org.uk/help-for-young-people/news-views/youth-index-2014

girls suffer from depression.[2] Teachers report rising rates of depression and anxiety among teenagers,[3] and hospital admissions doubled from 2013 to 2016.[4] Teenage girls are a particular worry, as they tend to turn their distress in on themselves, not drawing attention to their mental disturbance until it is well entrenched and much harder to treat.

While the statistics are sobering, I like to remember that the majority of teens are coping magnificently well despite the pressures. So although I want to stay alert to any signs that a girl needs extra support through her teens, I also celebrate the strength of our girls to withstand the stresses of adolescence.

In this chapter, I explore the reasons why there is such a striking inner change as our daughters leave their childhood and move into their teenage years. I seek to explain how a dangerous combination of factors results in an increasing number of our girls floundering because of their tendency to internalise their problems and blame themselves. Self-punishing behaviours are explained alongside case studies that illuminate and clarify what can happen. I discuss some of the cultural pressures that girls face, including those arising from social media and the tendency to focus obsessively on their body image. The chapter looks at the real definition of beauty and offers ways in which parents can help their daughters feel good about themselves. There is a Girl Talk section called 'How to lift your spirits' for teens who are feeling down, and I call attention to the fact that praise is not a helpful parenting tool.

2   Praveetha Patalay & Emla Fitzsimons, *Mental Ill-health Among Children of the New Century: Trends Across Childhood with a Focus on Age 14* (September 2017), Centre for Longitudinal Studies, London.
3   Rachel Rosen, '"The Perfect Generation": is the internet undermining young people's health?' (Parent Zone, 2016). https://parentzone.org.uk/sites/default/files/The Perfect Generation report.pdf
4   Geraldine Bedell, 'How has society managed to produce a generation of teenagers in which mental-health problems are so prevalent?', *Independent* (27 February 2016). http://www.independent.co.uk/life-style/health-and-families/features/teenage-mental-health-crisis-rates-of-depression-have-soared-in-the-past-25-years-a6894676.html

. . . .

We can change the trend of suffering for our teens.

. . . .

THE TEEN YEARS, A VULNERABLE STAGE . . .

- A baby girl reaches for her toes, fascinated as they dance in and out of her vision.
- A little girl pulls up her top to display her round belly proudly.
- A young girl dances up and down the hallway, delighting in her nakedness before a bath.
- A young schoolgirl insists on wearing the same worn T-shirt five days in a row because she adores it.
- A primary school girl tucks her skirt into her knickers to keep it out of the way while she climbs a tree.
- A young girl teeters along in her mother's silk dress and heels, pouting red lipstick and twirling in front of the mirror.
- A preteen girl arrives late to school on a non-uniform day after a meltdown over what to wear.
- A teenage girl disappears into the bathroom, to emerge two hours later with legs shaved, hair washed and straightened, face made up, short skirt, heels and smelling of a cocktail of beauty products. She pauses in front of the mirror, sucks her tummy in, and grimaces.
- A teenage girl sits at the table pushing her food around the plate. No one realises that she has already missed breakfast and skipped lunch.
- Another teenage girl never eats breakfast. She is trying to diet, but she's hungry. At bedtime she finds herself gorging on half a packet of biscuits and then feels bad.
- A teenage girl pulls off her skirt and tosses it to the floor where it joins the growing pile of discarded clothes. She holds up another and drops that too. She yanks on a pair of trousers, cannot fasten them, and bursts into tears.
- A young woman wraps a towel around her body and manages to wriggle out of her swimming costume and into her underwear without removing the towel.

- A young woman sits in front of the television, an empty crisp packet, ice-cream carton and biscuit tin before her. The phone rings – a friend suggesting to meet up – but she says no and goes back to watching the television.
- A woman frowns at her credit card statement – new outfit, hair tinting, foundation and mascara, magazine subscription, four-inch heels, cut and blow dry, face cream, wax, new bikini, gym membership, new dress – the list goes on for pages.
- A young mother serves dinner to her children and sits with them at the table nursing a cup of tea, trying to lose a stone – again.

What happens to us?

Teens are awash with feelings, often strong, conflicting and confusing. It's normal for this stage of life, and hopefully there will be support around to help them make sense of the swirl of emotions. (See Chapter Six.) A teenager's heartbreak is more painful than an adult's; her rage is more consuming; her fears are more paralysing; her joy is more exhilarating.

As children mature they become more aware of the world around them but are not necessarily able to manage their responses. Things happen that can be too much for them to handle: parents separate, pets die, grannies get frail, friends fight, romance ends, exams loom, they have a terrible haircut, a favourite sibling leaves home, there's a car crash, they move house, the list of endangered species grows, wars rage.

As if this isn't enough, teen brains are undergoing a substantial reconfiguration, which leaves them less able to think clearly for a few years. The break-up of a relationship brings to the surface how unloved and unlovable a teen feels. This is easily translated into thinking herself fat and ugly. A snarky comment from a friend demonstrates the fragility of friendships that are relied upon for self-worth, and a girl can quickly feel totally isolated and alone. A new purchase, an invitation or a compliment gives rise to a euphoric high – but more are needed to sustain it. Simultaneously it becomes less acceptable for her to resort to her childhood releases of sobbing, tantrums, shrieks of delight and shouts of frustration. Life is busier with fewer opportunities to spend relaxed time in the supportive company of women. Alongside this, she often enters a time of discord with her parents, just when she desperately needs their love and encouragement, so she finds herself turning to the immature advice of her peers. Friction with parents gives rise to huge insecurity, which must be hidden in a bid to prove independence.

For many teen girls their feelings are just too much to manage, so they seek an escape (as many adults do) through no fault of their own or their family. For others, having such strong feelings seems wrong and so they hide them, which can lead to depression.

The degree to which our girls are running into mental health difficulties suggests that it is worse for teens now than it was for us when we were their age.

ENDLESS PRESSURES AND SELF-HARM

The teenage years are often a time of great strain – a teenage girl wants to fit in but without losing herself, at the same time as dealing with the confusion of puberty, intense feelings, and a strong need to prove herself grown-up. And all the while her teachers want better work; her popularity is measured by likes on social media; online porn is creating norms and expectations within romantic relationships that make it harder than ever to say no; the world calls to her to be taller, thinner, groomed, gorgeous and have her feelings under control. Let's look at some of these pressures in more detail.

School. We rank our children by their grade and there is always pressure to do better. Children are anxious about future job prospects, as even university graduates no longer walk into jobs, apprenticeships are scarce, further training leads to student debt, and many young adults get stuck living at home with their parents.

Popularity. Teenagers orientate themselves strongly towards their peers, knowing at some level that they are approaching a time when they will be leaving their parents and siblings to make their own way in the world. With the internet there is no downtime, no excuse to be unavailable. Friends are forever awaiting a response, and their popularity is there for all to see – how many friends, likes, tweets, messages do they have?

Social media. Social media, reality television and the smartphone culture are creating serious mental health issues for teenage girls, as they allow and almost compel them to compare themselves daily with their peers and with unrealistic role models, contributing to a constant feeling that they are not good enough, pretty enough, popular enough, and that everyone else is having a much better time than they are. Social media can warp their understanding of sex and relationships, and distance them from a healthy sense of self.

Body image. We surround our girls with images of idealised female perfection. Just as they become more curvaceous and hair is growing in new places, they are also contending with spots, greasy hair, mood swings and self-consciousness. And, as if that isn't enough, they are bombarded with messages that they must work hard to get their bodies looking a certain way. Hair must be removed, coloured, straightened, styled. Skin must be clear, tanned, soft. Tummies flat, hips narrow, waist trim, legs long. With images now digitally altered, girls strive for a type of female beauty that is impossible to attain.

A damaging process can happen in the mind of a teenage girl: rather than seeing external stressors as the main culprit, she becomes fiercely self-critical. Rather than looking outside of herself for the reasons for her distress, she makes it her own fault. When we adults fail to reduce the pressures on our girls, they blame and often punish themselves as a way of coping. Rather than looking to others for support, they try to cope on their own, finding ways to numb overwhelming feelings.

One in ten sixteen-year-olds surveyed in a 2013 study at Queen's University Belfast had considered self-harm or taking an overdose: 'By far the most likely reason why young people self-harm remains self-punishment. This suggests that young people with mental health problems keep blaming themselves . . . rather than appreciating external stressors such as pressures arising from school work or financial difficulties.'[5]

The plague of perfectionism. Some girls just want to be perfect. They strive to be flawless, set themselves unattainable goals, constantly feel they fall short, and see mistakes as a sign of failure. Perfectionists tend to believe that they will only be liked if they do well. Aiming high can be rewarding and lead to success as long as a girl's self-worth isn't tied to her achievements. But perfectionism becomes a tyranny when it's driven by fear of failure and self-criticism. This makes school work stressful, relationships exhausting, mistakes hateful, and anything new a threat as she puts herself under so much pressure to get it all right. Her self-esteem is especially precarious and she needs us to keep an eye out for signs of depression or being overwhelmed.

Self-harming teens – why do they do it?

Cutting, starving, bingeing, burning, drinking, drugs, promiscuity: these are the most popular ways of self-harming. Many parents harbour a secret fear that the teenage years might bring these things. At the same time, parents assume that *their* child won't self-harm. We protect ourselves by believing that teens who turn to this behaviour come from other families, families with big problems, not families like ours. Sadly this isn't so. Self-harming is on the increase, predominantly in teenage girls, and is to be found in families of all backgrounds, all classes, all circumstances.

For those who have never experienced the high of self-harming, these behaviours can seem impossible to understand. There is a human coping mechanism of using self-inflicted pain to distract from an emotional pain that feels too overwhelming. When a girl's feelings become too

---

5   Queen's University Belfast (*2013 Young Life and Times Survey*). 'One in 10 16-year-olds have considered self-harm, study shows', *ScienceDaily* (16 May 2014)

much to bear, another more controllable pain provides relief. A sense of peace descends as the razor slices through her skin; thoughts of food (eating it or not eating it) take over from other more painful thoughts that otherwise circle round and round; drink or drugs temporarily numb her; sex takes over her mind for a short while, with the added benefit of feeling wanted, albeit briefly. Unbearable feelings that seem out of her control are calmed by exercising extreme self-control in some other area of life, whether it be food, pain or the opposite sex. To someone else it may seem as if the teen is out of control, but to her the deeply reassuring experience is of being *in* control. Unfortunately, parents of teenagers often make the mistake of focusing on the harmful behaviour and trying to change that, rather than addressing the root cause. The real way towards no longer needing the coping mechanism of self-harming is to explore the feelings of distress that lie behind the self-damaging behaviour.

Do not believe your daughter to be immune. No matter how happy you imagine her life to be, how stable her family, or how good her friends, do not assume that she can always handle the intensity of her teenage emotions. Use Mother–Daughter Dates to give her a break. Listen to her, really listen. And if you are going through a patch when closeness is tricky, persist; keep looking for ways of spending fun time together and make sure that you are not the only woman in her life who cares. Don't abandon her to the support of her peers only, but build a circle of women who are actively involved in her life and who she can turn to if you are not the right person for just now. And if your daughter is experiencing the urge to self-harm in any way, don't tackle it on your own; get professional support for her and for yourself.

Mia finds temporary relief in self-harming

Mia had been looking forward to starting secondary school. She was moving up with lots of her friends from primary school, they'd all be taking the bus together, and she'd be getting her own phone. She was a bit overwhelmed in the first week with so many different classrooms to find, different teachers for every subject, and so many unfamiliar faces, but she soon found her feet.

The trouble started in the second term: some of her old friends had formed a new cool crowd and they were leaving her out. Mia made the mistake of trying to get back in with them by posting on social media a group photo of them all from a few years back, but they made fun of her instead. She tried to joke back, but that made things worse. Then someone posted an old photo of her dressed as a princess at a fancy-dress party and it went around the school.

Taking refuge alone in the school library, Mia tried to get on with her homework. She felt so upset, so lonely, so picked on. 'Not fair', she gouged with the end of her compass on her notepad. Then, without knowing why, she stuck the end of the compass into the back of her hand, increasing the pressure until a bead of bright red blood appeared. A sense of calm descended on her. She watched the blood trickling slowly onto her page. The bell rang. She licked the blood from her hand and went to class.

This was the first of many times . . .

Sarah feels more in control when she doesn't eat

Sarah's parents were having a trial separation. Her mum was working longer hours to support herself and her two girls. Sarah missed her dad even though she saw him most weekends. She just wanted things to go back to how they were, but instead her mum and dad seemed to be fighting more. Her exams were fast approaching, but she couldn't seem to get down to any revision. She would wake up and for a moment would forget; then it would hit her that her parents were most likely getting divorced, and she just didn't feel like getting up. She'd leave it until the last minute, skip breakfast and run for the bus. The sick feeling in the pit of her stomach meant she often couldn't face the canteen at lunchtime. She liked the feeling of emptiness. Not eating gave her a feeling of control. Her friends noticed that she was getting skinny and said she looked good. Deep down Sarah feared that her parents' break-up might be her fault; she felt bad. Not letting herself eat was a kind of punishment. Concentrating on losing weight dampened her feelings of unhappiness. She got herself locked into a cycle of denying herself food and losing weight, which made her feel temporarily better but still fat so needing to lose more.

Six months later Sarah was taken into hospital morbidly underweight.

BODY IMAGE, FOOD AND REAL BEAUTY

Checking the mirror for changes

It's normal for a teenage girl to become absorbed with her own image. She is looking for herself. So many of the changes in adolescence are physical and they happen so fast – no wonder our teenagers check the mirror with such frequency: Who am I? Am I still me? Who am I becoming? Who could I be? A girl's appearance becomes inextricably linked in her mind with who she is.

A teenager's self-centredness is essential in her quest for establishing her identity. The mistake that teenagers make, because they are so focused on how they look, is that they imagine that everyone else is watching them too; hence their heightened self-awareness. We must be careful not to ridicule or minimise a girl's painful self-consciousness. Help your daughter by being a mirror to her. Enable your daughter to see herself by telling her how you see her strengths and capabilities.

Pause and consider how many times you tell her what she is doing wrong. Is this the mirror you want to be holding up to her? She will prefer the mirror that her friends present to her and turn to social media 'likes' for affirmation. Be mindful of your praise, too – children are highly attuned to the meaningless compliments dished out automatically by adults. What she needs from you is honest feedback. Next time you see her checking herself in the mirror, smile at her.

'Does my bum look big in this?'

Immersed in a culture that idealises looks, worrying about weight and appearance is so all-pervasive that we hardly question it. The focus ought to be on what creates this anxiety, not on how we can live with it or how we can reduce it by losing weight and altering our appearance.

My daughter is still young enough to inhabit her body in total comfort. It's not that she is not conscious of her body: she's deliciously aware of it. She delights in it. She likes to adorn it, change outfits several times a day, dance and run and jump and climb, wallow in a bath, snuggle under a fleecy blanket, and gleefully prance about. Her body is an uncomplicated source of pleasure for her. But something terrible is going to happen. She is going to learn to judge her body, to wish it were different, and probably to expend effort, time and money trying to alter it. No matter how much we love her, love the way she looks and let her know this, other forces are at work that will cut across all this and destroy her easy self-acceptance.

Before they even reach their teens most girls have a troubled relationship with their bodies. They worry about how they look, being fat, having hair in the wrong places, not being tanned, their skin, hair, nose and bum. Many teenage girls already have a regime of painting their faces, shaving and coiffing. Most girls have tried skipping meals and eating less in an attempt to be thinner. Children are fed a constant diet of images showing them how women are meant to look and behave. Greater importance seems to be given to how we seem and what we have, rather than what we do or who we are.

Women's bodies are used everywhere to sell cars, perfume and chocolate, on billboards, magazines and television. On the screen our heroines are slim, feminine and blemish-free. Models on the catwalk and in the shop window are dangerously underweight. Pop stars gyrate provocatively, and women depicted in computer games have taken Barbie to a whole new level of improbable proportion, peddling fake dreams of mastery, agility and sensuality. You see it without looking.

The boys are watching online porn and then want their girlfriends to re-enact what they have seen. They expect long, slender legs, big breasts, slim waist and no body hair. Women's bodies are revealed to sell all kinds of products, but frowned upon if seen breastfeeding. Women in the west have the lowest body-confidence, with few able to say they like their bodies. Girls who start out loving their big tummies and fascinating toes learn to judge and find fault with their figures. Life-threatening eating disorders are on the increase, and women mutilate their bodies, spending increasing millions on cosmetic surgery.

How you can help your girl to keep loving her body

- Take care of yourself with good food, sleep and exercise, increasing your body-esteem.
- Look at your body in the mirror with kind eyes.
- Exercise and eat for health rather than to lose weight.
- Never criticise your body in front of your daughter.
- Never criticise your daughter's body.
- Limit your spending on your appearance.
- Reduce your exposure to glossy magazines and celebrity gossip.
- Fill your life with real people.

Thus we liberate ourselves and our daughters too!

Stop photoshopping. Stop the tyranny for ourselves, for our daughters, for their daughters!

Photoshopping is making us miserable – it's impossible not to compare ourselves to the images that fill screens and magazines. It's encouraging our daughters to aspire to an impossible ideal. No diet, surgery or personal trainer can give the idealised shape with perfect skin that is routinely created by digital jiggery-pokery. Nevertheless, girls still diet, go under the knife, exercise fanatically, shave, straighten and cover with make-up.

It's killing our girls. Eating disorders have the highest mortality rate of any mental illness.

It's a crime against women – it's stealing our time, mental wellbeing, energy and money.

So we say STOP to photoshopping! We speak out, stop buying the magazines, stop buying the products that claim to beautify, stop dieting, and stop trying to change how we look to conform to some unattainable ideal. We complain to the regulatory bodies that are there to take note. We celebrate ourselves exactly as we are by wearing comfortable clothes and less make-up, and eating exactly what feels right.

She is gaining weight – should I say something?

No! Not unless you want her to worry about her weight her whole life long.

. . . .

Tell a girl she should watch her weight, and she is more likely to become fat.

. . . .

Knowing how harsh society can be towards overweight people, it's understandable when mothers try to protect their daughters by advising them to watch their weight. Sadly, this perpetuates the tyranny of 'never feeling slim enough' that many women carry their entire lives, and research shows it also raises the chances of a girl ending up heavier than if nothing was ever said.[6]

It's healthy for preteen girls to gain some weight as they enter puberty. A woman's body is not like a girl's body, so you would expect a girl to gain curves as she enters her teens. Some girls get wider before they get taller, and most will never again have the shape of a girl, a shape that is sadly idealised in the fashion and celebrity world.

Body image is how you *feel* about your body, not how well your body measures up to impossible ideals. Encourage your daughter to feel good about her body. Body comfort comes from eating well, sleeping well and exercising. It comes from feeling loved, cared for and accepted.

Junk food battles

A lot of teens like to eat junk food because it requires no effort and satisfies a craving; it feels comforting and can numb difficult feelings. Their bodies are changing rapidly and they don't know how to get the increased nutrients they need. Many don't understand how to manage PMS and food cravings. But junk food contains sugar and salt in quantities that are not good for their health.

If junk food is serving some of your teen's needs but you are worried about the long-term effects, there are two strategies that work better than nagging:

1. Stop worrying about the 'bad food' and concentrate on providing plenty of good food. A high-protein breakfast often leads to healthier food choices throughout the rest of the day.

6 Eric Robinson & Angelina R. Sutin, 'Children gain more weight when parents see them as "overweight"', *Psychological Science*, 28(3) (2017), 320–9.

2. Think about what junk food is giving your teen, and figure out other ways of meeting those needs:

- Is it hunger, or is it feelings, that has her reaching for the crisps or chocolate straight after school?
- Does she need a chat rather than a bowl of sugared cereal just before bed?
- In the lead-up to her period, would a hot bath and easing back on activities help her to avoid devouring a whole packet of biscuits?

You may need to start with yourself and gently tackle the reasons behind any comfort eating of your own so that you are modelling healthy behaviour to your teen.

What is beauty?

In Girls Journeying Together we ask ourselves what beauty is and who decides. I show the girls how the 'ideal' woman has changed over time, from Rubens' voluptuous lovelies painted in the seventeenth century and the curvaceous women of the 1950s to the skinny models of today. We also look at what women will do to their bodies in the pursuit of beauty: Chinese foot-binding, Burmese neck rings, African scarification, Elizabethan mercury face-whitening, and western plastic surgery. The girls realise that our ideals for feminine beauty depend on when and where you live.

The girls are excited to learn how to put on make-up, curious about when and how to remove hair, interested to talk about dealing with spots, greasy hair and sweaty armpits. They see these things as passports to womanhood.

What would your response be?

- She wants to shave at age nine after coming home in tears because someone called her hairy.
- She has gone from wearing a bit of eye make-up to adding lipstick

and blusher, and now she is insisting she needs foundation costing £50 a pot.

- Mornings before school are a stress of needing to wash and straighten her hair, put on 'her face', not having the right shirt, and refusing to wear her coat.
- There's a party and she wants a new top, new shoes and to have her hair styled.
- They do eyebrow threading in the mall – can she have a tenner?
- She wants a pair of heels that she can barely walk in.
- She hates her hair; she says she will feel better if next time she can have braids and extensions.
- Everyone's got braces; she wants veneers, or at least to get her teeth whitened.
- She wants a full wax because that's what her boyfriend likes and expects.

When your daughter wants something that shocks you, it tells you something about the culture she is living in, including the home culture.

In Girls Journeying Together girls think about all their favourite people and then consider how beautiful each one is to her and why. It becomes clear that true beauty is how you are in yourself, how you treat the people around you, and how you live – not what you look like.

WHAT PARENTS CAN DO TO HELP

When a child is struggling, our impulse is to try to make the suffering go away. That's only natural, but it's better to equip her to manage life's challenges. If you swoop in and try to fix it, you will give her the message that you don't think she is capable of finding a way to cope. Instead, take the opportunity to help her figure out how to tackle life when it gets her down. Then spend time doing something fun.

Teens tell me that they don't talk to their parents because their parents don't listen.

Take her seriously. Listen and listen some more. Children want to feel heard. They usually don't want advice, suggestions, a great long chat or a big lecture. They want to hear themselves think aloud and often will work out their own solutions, though maybe not in one go – you may have to leave her to mull it over (which may feel uncomfortable for you both). Don't assume it's resolved just because she is not talking about it; keep checking in to see how she is doing. Ask her what she thinks would help or who she feels would be a support. If it's more serious, find professional help.

Every time you interact with your daughter with love, you are supporting her. The way you talk to her becomes her inner voice. Each time you are able to empathise with her you help her to take her feelings seriously and to believe she can manage them. Although there may be times when your daughter's behaviour appals you, and you are more aware of her faults than anything else, still look for her strengths and her gifts. Hold in your mind that misbehaviour is often a sign of her suffering, and focus on what is good in her. Spare her from your comments about how tough she is to parent, and share them with your close friends instead. Never miss an opportunity to tell a teen girl what you like about her. She may squirm, but she will still hear you.

Many grown women are afflicted by not thinking highly of themselves, underestimating what they are capable of, running themselves down, dieting constantly and engaging in activities that block out their feelings. Let's interrupt that cycle. Figure out how to stay connected and communicating with your teen and show her how you care.

Teen suicide – too much pressure on our daughters

A precious fifteen-year-old girl tried to take her life today. The number of pills tells us this was no 'cry for help' – she meant it. She must have felt that she could no longer bear to live. Suicide is a leading cause of teen deaths according to the World Health Organisation and rates among young people have been increasing to such an extent that they are now the group at highest risk in a third of all countries. Thousands of adolescents take their lives every year and for every death there are twenty others attempting suicide.[7]

· ·

Girls often internalise their worries – rather than thinking there is something wrong with the world, they think, 'There must be something wrong with me.'

· ·

Our job is to protect and strengthen our girls. We need our teens to have a strong sense of self-worth and inner confidence, exactly at a stage when their confidence is often wobbling. They need our love and understanding, especially when their behaviour is harder to understand. Think of small, daily ways in which you can help your teenager to feel your love and acceptance. Don't wait, do it now, whatever your daughter's age. Ink your Mother–Daughter Dates into the diary. In Girls Journeying Together the girls discuss real beauty, true friendship, and the many routes to realising a dream. Encourage your daughter to question and challenge the accepted norms. Help her to know that good qualifications are not paramount, having a few really good friendships is key, and beauty is not found on the bathroom scales or in the changing room. Notice what *you* do in everyday life that gives credence to these beliefs. Building inner confidence takes time and comes with age. Teens need older women to befriend them, to mentor them at a time when they may not want to turn to their parents but still need adult guidance. We all need people who care.

Message to our fifteen-year-old friend

I am immeasurably glad that you are still alive. I am so sorry that life became too much to bear that day and I want you to

---

7   *Global accelerated action for the health of adolescents (AA-HA!): Guidance to support country implementation* (WHO, 2017). http://www.who.int/maternal_child_adolescent/topics/ adolescence/framework-accelerated-action/en/

know that I want to do anything that I can to help you on days like that, or any other day. But I also know how hard it is to reach out, especially when you're feeling low, so I hope that you can find ways to survive the times when it all feels unbearable. It won't go on forever, I promise; just do whatever you can to get through these really tough times. You will find your own unique way through. You have always done things your way, feisty in your independence, and smart in a way that exams cannot test. Although you can be loud and full of passion, I see that you are sensitive, easily hurt and feel things deeply.

I want you to live. I want you to feel like you want to live.

With my heartfelt love, Kim.

Praise makes her feel worse!

It's ingrained in many of us that praising is proper parenting behaviour, so it's a hard habit to break.

It starts with, 'What a clever girl – you ate all your greens!'

and goes on with, 'That's a brilliant picture!'

and on . . . 'You're a great teenager!'

and on . . . 'Really, you look perfect!'

and on . . . 'You're so kind, such a good friend!'

and on . . .

Praise can be experienced as patronising, paralysing and impersonal.

- We tend not to praise our adult friends in this way, as it seems patronising.
- Superlative praise is impossible to live up to and can be paralysing.
- General praise is meaningless, especially when dished out indiscriminately.

Although praise may temporarily give a boost, it often doesn't even do that. Children discount the superlatives and discard parents' opinions as biased. Praise can even make a child feel worse because it conjures up in their minds all the times when they aren't good, perfect or kind. We praise to please, bolster, motivate – and yet praise does the opposite of all three. Research shows that children who are praised perform less well and like themselves less. This may seem paradoxical at first, but when a child is constantly told how clever she is, the pressure to match up causes her to do less well. A group of children were set a maths test and afterwards half were praised and the other half were not. They were then set a harder test; not only did the praised group perform less well, but they lied about their results to make themselves sound better.[8]

Strong self-esteem does not come from someone else's compliments. If you come to rely on others' commendation for a sense of wellbeing, you become dependent on others for your sense of self, which then never feels solid. Real self-confidence comes from being truly seen and heard. A child can experience this when an adult clearly chooses to spend time with her, listens and pays attention. Any remarks the adult makes demonstrate the quality of the attention:

'You ate all your greens. Did you enjoy them?'

'Your picture has a lot of pinks, reds and oranges . . .'

'Now that you spend more time with your friends, our family mealtimes seem so precious.'

'You've done your hair differently today.'

'Your friends seem to call on you for support.'

8   Jennifer Henderlong & Mark R. Lepper, 'The effects of praise on children's intrinsic motivation: a review and synthesis', *Psychological Bulletin*, 128(5) (2002), 774–95.

• •

Praise ends conversations, while noticing and describing starts them.

• •

Parents who praise are often trying to make up for all the inconsiderate criticism that was cast around in their childhood. Now it's praise that is flung about, and this is just as damaging. If praising is a hard habit to break, start by observing; when you say something, be specific rather than general; describe what you see without passing judgement on it. You are holding a mirror up for your daughter to see herself. You may find that this initiates some really illuminating conversations.

Is she just a moody teenager?

A worried mother writes

'She's not right. I can't put my finger on it, she's just not her normal self. Seldom happy, like everything's a bit disappointing. She used to love gymnastics but she's given it up, to see her friends she said, but she's not doing that either now. She used to have such a laugh with her friends. That's what's bothering me. I've not seen her laugh in ages.'

A month later:

'I just thought that Catrina's moods were part of being a teen. I mean, she seemed okay mostly. A bit unmotivated maybe, a bit antisocial, but that's normal at that age, isn't it? She started staying up until all hours, but I've got problems sleeping too so I just thought she'd inherited that from me. I should have paid more attention when her school report showed a drop in all her grades, but they go through phases, don't they, kids? Next thing I know I'm in A&E and she's having her stomach pumped. I mean, why? I don't understand.'

It's easy to miss the warning signs, so trust your instincts. You know your daughter well; if you feel something's not right, then it probably isn't. Everyone is different: one person's depression looks just like another's natural introversion. One person's emotional turmoil appears like another's dramatic expression. If you follow your intuition about any changes in your child's demeanour, you will know if she needs extra support. Notice if her sleeping has changed, her diet, her pattern of socialising, her performance at school. Be alerted by her isolating herself, losing motivation, gaining or losing weight, drinking, being agitated or restless, panicking if separated from social media, getting overly tired, not caring about anything, suffering from ongoing sadness, losing control, engaging in precocious sexual activity, or getting into trouble with the law. Check in with others who know her well. Create opportunities for her to talk to you, knowing she still may not be able to. Don't ignore the warning signs – take unusual behaviour seriously and look for support from friends, professionals, child helplines and online. Girl Talk – How to lift your spirits gives simple directions for girls who are suffering.

Girl Talk – How to lift your spirits

Most people experience depression at some point in their lives, so lots of research has been done on how to recover your sense of wellbeing. There's no one-size-fits-all quick fix for feeling down, but there's a range of things that we know help. A lot of it is common sense, but nevertheless it works; and although it sounds simple, that doesn't mean that it's always easy. You will recognise a lot of the things on this list as the boring stuff your parents nag you to do. There's a reason for that: these things really do help people to feel well. You don't need to do everything on the list – just start small and choose the easiest one for you.

Be kind to yourself

There's a really good reason why you feel down, even if you don't know what it is, so be kind to yourself. You may find you get easily overwhelmed or anxious, with little energy for doing things, so make life simpler for a little while if you can. Don't feel bad – it's not your fault that you feel this way. It won't last forever. Day always follows night. Where there's a shadow there's always light. Hang in there.

Sleep

If you don't get enough sleep your body will be slower – slower at thinking, slower at sport, slower at healing and slower at sorting out feelings. People who don't get enough sleep report feeling more moody, irritable or anxious. They find it harder to concentrate or get motivated and are more likely to have bad skin, crave unhealthy food and find it hard to get to sleep. Lots of things help with sleep. Mostly it's about routine: bath, book, music, warmth – whatever helps you to get relaxed.

However, if you sleep too much you will also feel sluggish and slow. Get up!

Wash

You may not feel like taking care of your body when you feel down, but you'll feel worse if you don't. A shower can help to get you going and you will smell better too.

Exercise

Physical movement releases feel-good brain chemicals. The hardest step is the first one, especially if you're feeling low and lethargic. Choose something you used to enjoy like cycling, skating or dancing. Or just start with walking somewhere.

Eat healthy food

Sugar, cakes, biscuits, white bread, pasta, processed foods don't help despondency. If you want to lift your mood, you need to avoid blood sugar highs, because they only lead to lows; this means don't miss meals, and eat a good breakfast. Give yourself lots of protein at the start of the day and eat those green things. You will feel better for it.

Sunshine

Get some. On your face, especially in the darker months; it helps to get rid of winter blues.

Quiet times

Sometimes the best thing you can do for yourself is to take some time to be alone. Not moping, but actually asking yourself what is at the bottom of this feeling glum. Be honest with yourself. Are you angry deep down? Or when you feel anxious, what is really frightening for you? Or has something saddened you? Listen to your self-talk, the things you say to yourself, to hear what is going on inside you. Some people find writing, drawing or music helps them to discover what's inside.

Friends and family

It can be tempting to keep to yourself when you feel down, but then you end up feeling worse – isolated and lonely. Being around people, the right people, can help you not to sink too low. You want to seek out the love and affection that's out there for you, especially when you're not feeling it too much for yourself.

Animals

Animals have special powers of understanding. If you don't believe me, go and spend some time with a dog, cat, bunny, chicken, horse, llama, guinea pig – well, maybe not a chicken.

Expressing feelings

This takes courage, and lots of adults find it hard too. It could be that no one's going to be able to change things for you, but talking about it and having someone listen can change how you feel about things. Counsellors are trained to help people figure their way through difficult patches. Another thing that can help is to turn your feelings into art – for example painting, dancing or writing song lyrics.

The meaning of life

You might be wondering about this now anyway. When you feel low it's a good time to sort out some priorities. What is the most important thing to you? What is the purpose of life – and of your life in particular? If you are struggling with the answers to these questions, then you are not alone. People have been pondering them for hundreds of years and have come up with some pretty good answers too, so if you are stuck for spiritual guidance, read some of what has been written; or if you belong to a religion or other community, talk to some of your elders. **If you ever think about ending your life, then take that feeling seriously: if you are in the UK, phone Childline (0800 1111) or the Samaritans (116 123) immediately, or for helplines in other countries contact Befrienders Worldwide (www.befrienders.org).**

Avoid addictive things

Anything that numbs your feelings only ever makes things better briefly. It doesn't sort the feelings out. So it's fine to distract yourself with a screen, dodge homework by staying out, or ease anxiety with a drink – but if it becomes a habit it will just add to your problems.

Self-talk

Say nice stuff to yourself sometimes. It's easy to get into a habit of being down on yourself, your life and everything around you, but that's never going to make you feel good. Choose not to do that. Even if it's only once a day, notice something good.

Help someone else

Someone else probably needs your help – an elderly person, a young parent, a pet owner or your parent. You will feel better about yourself too.

CHAPTER EIGHT

Her circle of women

Girls look to the women in their lives to give them a sense of what it is like to be a woman. They emulate the women they like and strive to be different from those they dislike. Many girls find themselves with only one woman who knows them well – their own mother. They rarely have the opportunity to hear women speak of their dreams, passions, relationships and bodies. And yet we expect our girls to find their own futures, know what is important to them, discover what they love to do, form firm friendships and like themselves.

Every girl needs women and the company of other girls with whom to learn about womanhood. A circle of female support to see her safely through her adolescence. Some girls are lucky enough to live in a community that naturally provides this female support, but many are not so fortunate.

In this chapter, I explore the concept of circles of women of all ages – mature female guidance to support our girls as they journey into and through their teen years. There is also the thread that we women recreate through the generations: that of being a maiden who becomes a woman who becomes a wise crone. Each lending a hand to the others, sharing the strengths that each age brings and mentoring the ones who come after us. This is my dream. A world where a girl understands her place in the bigger and comforting picture of life, knowing that there is support from the community in her acquiring the whole range of life skills that she will need and having her maturing acknowledged. In turn, she will contribute to the next generation – becoming in this way part of a compassionate society where women help each other along; everyone being witness, guide and partner in celebration at different times of life.

Find mentors for your daughter and help her to join girls' groups such as Girls Journeying Together. When families have busy lives, live far from extended family, and children spend most of their time in the company of other children, a mentored girls' group can fill the gap providing guidance and community.

WHO IS IN YOUR VILLAGE?

Raising children is a task for all the community. No child was ever supposed to get all her rearing from just one or two adults, and no parents were ever supposed to bring up their children on their own. They say it takes a whole village to raise a child . . .

We all need elders, people who have the wisdom of having experienced and seen a lot and aren't afraid to speak out. Our daughters need aunties, godmothers and family friends to get a sense of the many different ways a woman can live her life. They need women who don't have children of their own. They need older teens who have only just been there themselves. They need younger girls to bring out their mentoring skills. And they need each other, girls at the same stage of life, to journey with them. Alongside this circle of women, we need the men and the boys.

Children like community. They are reassured by the feeling of belonging and they like the security of having a range of adults involved in their lives. Unfortunately, our culture is one of not interfering in the lives of other people's offspring, and so children have fewer adults playing an active part in their upbringing. We no longer know everyone in our neighbourhood, we often live a distance from extended family, apprenticeships are rare, and disciplining a child who is not your own is frowned upon – children are not seen as the joint responsibility of every adult around.

Can you remember a teacher, neighbour, auntie or family friend who touched your life deeply? Consider who the corresponding people might be in your daughter's life and how you might support the development of their relationship. In adolescence, peers are crucial – what they think, say and do. But don't let peers become the main influence in your daughter's life. Give her mature influences too, in you and in other older women.

Life with children can easily revolve around their timetables and their socialising, but a child's life that includes meaningful relationships with other adults is a rich one. As families move around more, we may have to make an effort to find our village wherever we go. It takes time for relationships to grow and for trust to build. Creating a sense of community supports the whole family.

Sasha finds female support next door for her daughter

Sasha learned at Rites for Girls of the importance of community, but her life was so full of work, kids, house and husband that she barely had any time for her own friendships, let alone for building up a network of women for her twelve-year-old daughter, Evie. Then they moved house, and by luck their new neighbour, Willow, turned out to be a great friend to both of them. Evie got to know her first because she lost her key and waited at Willow's for her mum to come home; she found Willow easy to talk to and poured out the difficulties she was having with fitting into her new school. Sasha popped over with some flowers to thank Willow and came home two hours later, as the two women got chatting. Willow used to be a photographer and helped Evie with her art project; Sasha cut Willow's hair every month; Evie helped Willow to use the internet; Willow sent Evie home with a batch of chocolate brownies; Evie sat with Willow when her pet dog died; Willow passed on her favourite books for Sasha to read; Willow was the second person Evie told when her period started.

Briony and Melanie's mothers didn't let the miles separate their girls

Briony and Melanie's mothers had done an antenatal course together. They lived down the street from one another, and the two girls had grown up going to the same nursery and primary school. When Melanie's family had to move to another town for work, both mothers recognised the importance of the bond and made sure to arrange weekends away for all four of them once or twice a year. Over the years both girls had times of trouble, but they always had each other and both mums to turn to.

MENTOR ME!

Adolescence is a time when a girl needs to have someone older she can talk to, someone who's not her mother. This is not because there's anything wrong with her own mother, or with their relationship – it's just that many girls want the distance that another woman brings.

The girls in Girls Journeying Together have taught me the importance of having mentors, even for those who have close relationships with their mothers. All girls have things that they choose not to share with their mothers, or at least not straight away, preferring to tell me or another woman or to discuss it in our girls' group instead.

There is something so personal and intimate about going through puberty. It's natural for a girl to feel private – to want to hold it close while she grows accustomed to the newness. Girls may not want those close to them to be involved, not just yet. At the same time they still want the reassurance of talking to someone who cares. This is where a mentor is of such benefit, not to replace a mother, but to offer 'other-motherness'. The relationship between mentor and girl will be as varied as the variety of women who take a mentoring role. It can be soft and gentle, feisty and fun, tough and confronting, cool and casual. It can give a girl the chance to hear her own thoughts, figure out her own solutions, test out her own ideas, rehearse how she might express herself to others, feel wisely supported, be tenderly challenged, be close to a woman who is not her mother.

Having a mentor or two gives a girl the sense that she has someone else looking out for her, someone interested in her, someone she can turn to. While it can be fun to follow the movements of a favourite pop idol or movie star, and women in the media can be very inspiring, there are real and special women who live in our own neighbourhoods who touch our children's lives. Ask your daughter; you may be surprised to discover who is inspiring and supporting her – a kindly neighbour, generous teacher or auntie. Delicately help your daughter make the most of the special women she has in her life.

Often you will need to invite the person into the role of mentor. Give them your permission to be involved by letting them know how important they are to your daughter and how much you appreciate their input. Make sure your daughter can spend time or be in touch with them.

Ideally, your daughter will grow up with an expanding circle of women around her, women who she comes to know and trust. Hopefully, having experienced the support of mentors, your daughter will, in turn, take a special interest in a girl younger than herself, and so the cycle continues . . .

Lydia's mum asks her sister to take a special role in Lydia's life

Lydia and her mum, Jane, had always been close. Lydia always told her mum if anything was troubling her, but lately she'd been less forthcoming. She began to shut her bedroom door and hide her texts, something she'd never done before. Jane wondered if this was normal teenage behaviour. When she asked other mothers, it seemed that it might be. Nevertheless, Jane recognised that the growing distance might feel as uncomfortable to Lydia as it did to her, so she thought about who else Lydia might feel able to talk to. Lydia had always got on well with her Aunt Julie, Jane's younger sister, even though they didn't see her very often. Jane talked to Julie and asked her if she would make contact with Lydia. Julie connected with Lydia on social media and made a point of visiting whenever she passed nearby. Jane bought them tickets to see a show together and drove Lydia over to stay with Julie one weekend. All this helped Lydia to become even closer to her aunt, who remained a source of support right through her adolescence and beyond.

A family friend helps Ella get back on track

Ella was bored at school and fell in with a crowd who were larking about and skipping lessons. She was a bright girl, so at first she was able to get away with it. But then she missed an important science practical, and the teacher alerted her parents by email. Ella claimed the teacher had given her the wrong room number. Ella's mum only found out the full extent of Ella's change in attitude to school when she bumped into Ella's old best friend in the newsagent's. Instead of confronting Ella, her mum invited a favourite family friend, Mary, to stay for the weekend. Mary brought chocolates, which she produced after Ella's parents had gone to bed, sharing them with Ella as they sat up late chatting. Mary asked about school, and when she responded sympathetically to Ella's initial complaint of it being boring, she heard more about how Ella couldn't see the point in what they were learning and realised that she needed more academic challenge. Mary told Ella's parents, who went to see Ella's tutor, changing the school's perception of Ella from a problem student to one who needed to be stretched.

Katy is close to her neighbour

When Katy's best friend stole some sweets from the shop around the corner, Katy felt bad about it but didn't know what to do. She didn't want her best friend to get into trouble. She talked to her neighbour, a young mother ten years older than her, and although the neighbour didn't have all the answers, she always had time to listen to Katy, and she helped her to figure things out.

Inspiring girls

What makes your heart sing? Could you share it with a girl you know?

Take time to share your passion with a daughter, niece, neighbour's girl or god-daughter. Pass on your interest and your knowledge.

Think back over your life and remember an older woman who inspired you. You could be that woman for some young girl now. The gift will not only be from you to her – you will be richer for giving it.

Each woman reach one, each woman teach one. Small changes can make a big difference.

MAIDEN, MOTHER, CRONE

After we met at a seminar, I joined three women in our local café. Just as we were ordering our tea and cake, one of the women suddenly waved the waitress over with great urgency for some water. Her face was pink and glistening and she seemed bothered.

'Hot flush?' one of the others asked sympathetically.

'Yes, a really strong surge,' she replied.

I felt curious – these older women belonged to a club that I would one day join.

Rather shyly I asked, 'What does it feel like?'

Prompted by my tentative questions, they talked about their experience of menopause. I'd been rather dreading the loss of my reassuring cycle, and the possibility of dealing with hot flushes, mood swings and sleeplessness – but the stories they told of the transformative effect it had in their lives made it suddenly sound very appealing.

With this precious experience of having my way ahead illuminated by three older women, I was even more committed to enabling this for our teenage girls everywhere and began to dream of training women to facilitate groups of Girls Journeying Together all over the world, and the Rites for Girls International Facilitator Training was launched.

In Girls Journeying Together, after we grow comfortable with each other, the girls enjoy talking about periods. They want to know what it feels like, whether it hurts and what to do if they start away from home. I invite an 'old girl' back to talk about what it's like having her period. I teach the girls about our monthly cycle, what to do about cravings and cramps, and the different ways to catch the blood. Another day we invite their mothers to join us so that the girls can hear a diverse range of women talk of their first blood and what their monthly cycles are like. It's natural for a prepubescent girl to feel ambivalent about her period starting – she is daunted by what she hears, as well as eagerly wanting the sign it provides of her growing up.

. . . .

At every stage of life our elders have so much to offer us.

. . . .

GIRLS JOURNEYING TOGETHER

Belonging to a girls' group during puberty can be enormously supportive to mothers and daughters alike. Every spring I start the year-long Girls Journeying Together groups, and a dozen ten- to twelve-year-olds sit in a circle in my sitting room nervously wondering how we will pass the afternoon. We have great fun preparing for puberty over a year of meeting monthly (so they gain a sense of what monthly feels like). In a calm, safe and supportive circle of girls, they share their apprehensions, misconceptions and discoveries. We talk about friendship problems and first dates, sanitary pads and cramping, photoshopping in fashion and epilators, dreams for the future and how to hold onto the uniqueness of self in the face of peer pressure and parents. Each girl identifies for herself what makes her special, and they support one another on their journey towards becoming spirited women full of character. The camaraderie that grows over the year shows them the strength that comes from girlfriends, and the girls form life-long friendships. Here is some feedback from girls who belong to Girls Journeying Together:

'At first I didn't think I'd like it, but it's brilliant. We talk about things, really talk, so you realise that others feel the same way.'

'I was nervous about growing up – I'm not now.'

'We've had loads of fun and learned stuff, but it hasn't felt like learning.'

'It got me thinking about who I want to be – what I want to do with my life.'

Their needs and concerns help to determine their year's programme, so each group is different. Over the year each girl can:

- Learn about the changes that puberty brings.
- Discuss the influences of peers, media, culture and parents.

- Prepare for her first period and find mutual support at bleeding time.
- Get to know the others really well – well enough to dare to speak her innermost fears and heartfelt hopes – and be known herself.
- Dream into her future.
- Clarify her values.
- Talk of spots, dating, falling out, exams and any other preteen concerns.
- Laugh, cry, play and feast.
- Find mentors.
- In time become a mentor herself.

We create a place where each girl is encouraged to be herself, to dress, speak and be true to however she is that day. The girls learn how to accept each other and experience what it's like to feel accepted by a group of peers. A year later we invite the mothers to join us for a celebration. Here are some things mothers have said about the group:

'My little girl seems so sure of herself, and I know that girls' group has been a huge part of that. I wish I'd had this when I was growing up.'

'Girls' group has transformed my relationship with my daughter.'

'My daughter just started her period and she was so calm and excited, and I knew how to manage it with her. A real gift from Girls Journeying Together group.'

'I wasn't sure about having another woman involved so intimately in my daughter's growing up, but if only I'd known how much girls' group would give her, and me, I'd never have had a moment's hesitation in bringing her along.'

CHAPTER NINE

The emerging woman – how to celebrate your daughter growing up

Teenagers crave our acknowledgement that they are growing up; they need us to guide them in their journey to adulthood and to notice that they are changing. Sadly, in our culture we have forgotten how to support them in this way through these pivotal and defining years. Celebrating your daughter's development is an important process and a powerful tool in supporting her to mature wisely and healthily. In this chapter, I briefly discuss the problems that we inherit due to the lack of celebratory rites for our girls as they move to womanhood. I describe the value of rituals and rites of passage for family life. I then provide stories from around the world of girls' puberty rites of passage to get you thinking about what would suit your daughter. Finally, I describe in detail all the elements necessary to co-create a tailored and meaningful rite of passage to celebrate your daughter's transition from childhood to adulthood.

It is important to remember that this is a lengthy process that requires your time, love and willingness to engage with your daughter. The stronger the connections between her and her family, circle of friends and circle of women, the deeper the message that she is being held and loved through a time when she does indeed need us all.

This chapter can guide you if you hold any of the following wishes:

- Do you feel like you want to do more to support your daughter through her teen years – but are not sure how best to?
- Do you want to mark the occasion of her first bleed – but feel certain that she'd sooner not?
- Do you want to mark the specialness of your daughter's growing up – but need to figure out some way of celebrating that she'd be comfortable with?

OLDER CULTURES KNEW IT

Human beings have always created meaningful ways to acknowledge and share important life events. Across cultures and continents our ancestors did and we still do. Rituals and ceremonies evolve to celebrate and support life transitions – into life, into union and out of life. However, there is one major life transition that now goes largely unattended: the transition from childhood to adulthood. In some cultures, and in times past, this was the transition that was given the most attention, as it was recognised as being the most crucial to get right. It was the one that needed the most input from others in the community, both for the sake of the young people and for the good of the community. Paradoxically it is the one that is now most often lost.

It used to be that children were prepared for adult life by their elders, culminating in a ceremony to mark their shift away from childhood. Even though some cultures still offer this rite of passage – Jewish bat mitzvah, Christian confirmation, Native American vision quest – we have very few common practices or culturally expected and accepted ways to ensure that we assist our girls to grow into strong young women. Nor do we have much to offer our boys to guide them towards becoming fine young men.

Although initiation into adulthood is no longer part of our culture, there's a lot to be gained by taking the essence from old customs and making new rites of passage to suit modern times.

Adolescence is extended in twenty-first-century western societies. We stay at school for longer, postponing the start of paid employment; we move out, pair up and have children later. The indicators of adulthood are delayed and our teenagers have fewer opportunities for affirmation from their adult communities of their right to be recognised as grown-ups.

Many teenagers have some ambivalence about growing up, and they flip-flop between behaving with maturity and behaving like toddlers; but nature compels them to grow up. It can be a confusing time. They want to know that we see that they are maturing, and if we don't give them this acknowledgement they will seek it out for themselves through mimicry of what they perceive to be 'adult behaviour'. At its best this can be taking on some new responsibility, caring for a friend in some way, or finding the courage to do things they couldn't do when they were younger. At its worst, it can be by trying to act like adults – in what they wear, watch, drink or do. Teenage risk-taking behaviours are often attempts at self-initiation to prove the reaching of adulthood.

. . . .

Young people crave their maturation to be acknowledged.

. . . .

Nowadays, we leave our children to navigate their way through a confusion of conflicting influences with little by way of systematic guidance. We miss the opportunity to influence positively their shaping into adults. While a teenager's brain is transforming, she is malleable and vulnerable. Young people benefit hugely from the guiding influence of honourable and caring adults. Many teens have only their parents to turn to during their times of challenge and change (and sometimes not even them).

Many girls lose motivation in their teenage years, fail to find the point in their studies, have difficulties in their friendships, choose less than ideal romance, have problems with eating or drinking, experiment with drugs, take risks, dress provocatively, struggle with the stress of exams, spend hours on screens, or feel depressed.

Too many teens are left to support one another and forge their own rites of passage. We leave our young people to band together and guide one another into adulthood. Many adults are intimidated by teenagers, and our culture of peer group supremacy makes parents hesitate to involve themselves. When no adult takes on this guiding role, the media tells teens how a man or woman should be and our youngsters look to each other for affirmation. We abandon them to a long, drawn-out adolescence if we fail to enable them to take over the reins and begin to adopt the attributes of a maturing grown-up.

We adults can take back the role of initiating our children into adulthood. In my experience, the children welcome it, we are fulfilled by it, and a transition that has become defined by its difficulty can become a more joyous one.

RITUALS TRANSFORM SOMETHING ORDINARY INTO SOMETHING SACRED

We already have all manner of family rituals to mark the passage of time and celebrate special changes – birthdays, graduations and anniversaries. Rituals provide structure and meaning to our everyday lives. We have bedtime rituals, rituals around food and personal hygiene. Some people do roughly the same thing every time they leave or enter their home, on Sunday mornings, when they have any kind of test, when saying goodbye or when signing off texts. Daily habits are the everyday rituals that liberate us from having consciously to decide each time how to do things, and they anchor us by providing a sense of order.

There are also extraordinary rituals or rites of passage used as a conscious acknowledgement of a life change. These encourage us to pause and pay attention; the ordinary flow of life stops and we are able to stand back and view our lives afresh. We may see more clearly what has meaning for us and what distracts us from our true purpose. Rites and rituals help us to shift our self-perception, enabling us to mature.

Rituals can be public, private or secret; planned or spontaneous. They do not always need words, witnesses or ceremony – some of the most powerful rituals are solitary and reflective. Rituals are timed by beats of the heart, not ticks of the clock, and should never be hurried.

Family rituals – to handle challenges and celebrate change

Rituals help us to make a transition easier, whether it be creating good endings, buying a first bra, starting a new year at school or leaving school. Notice the rituals you already have, and make others to support important changes within your family. And be sure to mark the significant shifts with a special something. I provide a few examples below.

Good endings. We can't always have happy endings, but we can have good ones. All around the world endings are ritualised. We know we need to say goodbye to our loved ones when they die, with a funeral or other reverential honouring. We have all manner of ways to sign off in our written communications: 'Yours sincerely', 'Kind regards', 'Love from'. Even texts and emails often end with a Xx or ♥. When we part we have a range of leave-taking rituals, from a handshake to a hug, a kiss and a wave: 'See ya!' 'Bye!' We know the importance of making an ending. We have ritualised ways that reflect our culture and the situation. Waving goodbye is one of the first gestures that we teach our babies.

We encounter many important endings throughout our lives and how these are handled can make a big difference to how we approach life. Endings are often not easy, and an adult's discomfort can mean that children are denied the full expression of their feelings. The last breast or bottle feed, growing out of a favourite item of clothing, the last day of term, the last day of the holidays, a change of teacher, the arrival of a sibling (and the end of life without), moving house, the death of a pet, a good friend moving away, parents' separation, the death of a grandparent, the end of a romantic relationship – all these can have a lasting impact on a young person. We expect the big things to affect them, but we often ignore those things that seem to us less dramatic. But to a child, and especially to a toddler or teenager (both of whom are undergoing rapid changes), small things can carry huge symbolic weight and are felt acutely. If we can resist the urge to minimise and 'make things okay', but instead help our children to explore the full range of their feelings towards endings in their lives, then they will approach subsequent endings with greater strength and less fear.

We know that providing a space for an ending to be acknowledged – celebrated, even – promotes wellbeing and a healthy society. Everyone has a different response to change. Often, though, if a child has regularly had her feelings ignored at times of significant change, or has been excluded from the marking of endings, she won't welcome change. Unexpressed feelings have a way of bubbling up later on, often inappropriately or inexplicably. So the child who was not allowed to miss a day of school with grief at the death of a beloved pet is less able to handle losing a boyfriend or girlfriend later on. And the child who was encouraged only to express excitement at the prospect of moving house is more likely to resist a new dish at dinner or the opportunity to try a new activity.

In the same way that cultures have rituals to help people deal with changes, families have their own small ways of creating good endings. We need not be shy of marking times of change with a simple ritual: it's a healthy way to move through the constant change of life. The art is in not overdoing it, making it over-precious or awkward for those present. Just as we would never walk away from someone without saying goodbye, we also acknowledge other endings without needing to make too big a deal of it. Creating rituals for teens is especially delicate, as they have heightened sensitivity to artifice and are easily embarrassed.

- A friend moving away could be marked by a special meal, with a card and gift on leaving.
- A pet can be buried in the garden, with something to mark the spot, and a few words said.
- A special smaller person could be chosen for the favourite item of clothing to be passed on to.
- You could blow giant bubbles and watch them float away to mark the last breast or bottle feed, the last day of school, the end of something special.

- Letters can be burned, or bundled up with a ribbon, to mark the end of a romance.
- The light from a candle can be blown out to say goodnight, goodbye to holidays, or farewell to a lost toy.
- Friends can gather around food, fire or a favourite haunt to wish one of them farewell with words of belonging, hope, affection and sadness.

One of the girls in Girls Journeying Together was leaving the country. Before our final meeting I asked the other girls in the group each to write a farewell message, really considering the girl to whom she was writing it (so no greeting card platitudes) and to bring a flower from her garden for her to press and take with her. Towards the end of our session each girl read out her card and gave her flower. I suggested they touch hands before moving back to their places in the circle and for some this became an embrace. We finished by blowing out the group candle and sending our love to go with her on her travels. A good ending was made.

First bra – a special occasion. Was getting your first bra a memorable experience? I hope so. A girl's first bra is a significant step along her path towards womanhood. She is introduced to a whole new world of lingerie choices: cup size, cotton or lace, black, white or skin-tone, underwired, padded, strapless, matching knickers. Be there to guide her into this new territory. Make an occasion of it rather than just popping into a department store on your way back from school. Take your lead from her – if she is excited, share her excitement; if she doesn't want to make a big deal out of it, play it cool. Recognise that it's a significant first purchase, however she may seem. Set aside some 'mother and daughter' time and perhaps go somewhere for cake afterwards. Make the acquisition of your daughter's first bra a cherishable memory.

Sophie starts an annual bra shopping tradition

Sophie's daughter was growing up; puberty was on its way. Sophie always bought her bras from the local department store, but it was very public and she wanted to find her daughter somewhere a bit more special for her first bra fitting. 'Why not make it a day trip to London and have a fitting at Selfridges?' her friend encouraged her, 'and let's try it out ourselves first.' The women had the best time, trying on bras they would never dream of wearing but also discovering that each had been wearing the wrong size. They learned things they never knew about bra variations and each treated herself to a perfectly fitting bra, a bit fancier than normal but not costing much more than they would usually pay. It was a revelation – and never too late to get it right.

A few months later Sophie took her daughter. Her daughter expected it to feel awkward, but she was pleasantly surprised. She felt a bit posh, but she loved it! Tea afterwards was a success too. This started an annual tradition for mother and daughter to go on a bra shopping expedition.

New school year. Every family has their rituals at the start of a new school year whether they realise it or not. It helps with the nerves and the excitement of more advanced work, new teachers, perhaps even a new school. Our little rituals help to prepare us: checking the uniform fits, replacing the broken lunch box, buying school shoes and a new pencil case, sorting through books, setting the alarm clock. Every child has different needs as they approach a new start. Parents will often instinctively offer the right kind of help for their child to make the shift from summer holiday mode into a new term.

As well as the practical preparations, you could find a way for your child to centre herself mentally before school starts. Invite her to pick three things that she wants to get out of her time at school this year. These are to be her three intentions, nobody else's, and it can be to do with anything from work, to friends, herself or after-school activities. Find a time when you can chat privately: this could be in the car or over cupcakes. It can be fun, informal and brief. Listen, encourage; she may not be used to thinking this way, so tease it out of her. Don't use it as a time to propose what you believe should be her goals, but sum up for her what you have heard her say. Suggest that she write her wishes down and seal them into an envelope that you will keep safe; then post this back to her six months later. School is an institution: the government decides the curriculum, and the teachers decide the lesson plan; your child can still decide how she is going to make the most of what is on offer.

Even if it seems strange the first time around, and a little false or forced even, I find that children come to want to repeat the exercise at the start of the next school year. That's how rituals work – they are out of the ordinary, but we soon adopt them and miss them if they are forgotten, using them to mark the passage of time and assist us in dealing with life's changes.

Not ready for big school? After the holidays – big school! It's presented as a big-new-exciting-thing, as new things often are to children. It reassures parents to hear their child expressing anticipation and readiness for change, but it's normal for children not to feel this way. Whether it's moving up to big school, starting her period, becoming a teenager, or any other big step in life, it's natural for a child to feel ambivalent. Children need to be reassured that feeling unsure of your readiness does not mean you are not ready. If you allow your child to voice her fears, ultimately this will allow her to make the transition.

End of school, end of an era . . . Leaving a school is an important milestone. All too often these transitions go uncelebrated and the opportunity for boosting your daughter is lost, perhaps at a time when she really needs it as she leaves what she knows and embarks on something new.

Each of us wants our daughter to feel good about herself, and making something of important events in her life can help towards this. It gives her the message that although a million others are going through this change at this time, you recognise that it's a big deal.

· ·

Her life is significant and important, particularly to you.

· ·

RITES OF PASSAGE AROUND THE WORLD

Puberty rites and coming-of-age ceremonies are still celebrated around the world. Sadly, we often associate them with mutilations, drug use or cultural practices we cannot understand out of context. Over time some have also become diluted, commercialised or rejected by the young people for whom they are intended.

Using my research into puberty rites, I have written fictionalised accounts of rites from different countries and religions to give you a flavour of them. Despite their wide differences, you will see some common themes that will guide you in knowing what might be important to include in a rite of passage for your daughter.

Rites of passage can be simple, not at all bizarre, and are a precious way of assisting our girls healthily towards strong womanhood. We can learn much from those who are still honouring these rites, and glean a great deal from how they were carried out in the past. We then need to adapt them to suit our culture and our girls.

Ama's Story

My name is Ama. My people are the Urubu-Ka'apor and we live in Brazil on the banks of the river Amazon. I am fourteen years old. Last week my bleeding began and so now I am in my *kapyk* at my home where I must stay alone for one moon cycle until my next bloods. This is my sacred preparation time. I can hear the sounds of my family in the main part of our home, but I cannot see them because they have hung palm-leaves to separate me. I miss playing with my sisters. I must stay in my hammock and not let my feet touch the ground, to keep the magic in me. My mother brings me food and warm water to bathe in. The warm water is nice; usually we wash in the river. The food is not too good though. I am only allowed *u'i* and *jaxi te*, cooked white cassava meal and stewed white tortoise. Yesterday my father cut all my hair off and I will only be allowed other foods when my hair has grown again. I am spinning my *carauá* string; my mother has shown me how. When I join the village again I will give some of my string to each of my relatives and the rest will be tied around my neck with feathers, like the other women in my village wear. Every day the women come to teach me. They bring sacred objects and tell me our stories. They are preparing me for my marriage to Tapu, our head goatsman. My mother says he'll be kind to me, but I feel sad to leave my home. I will have new duties, duties of a wife.

Next week my father will put *tapia'æ*, ants, onto my skin under cloth binders around my stomach and forehead. They will bite me, but I will show my *pyratã*, my strength; I will not cry out. The pain will make me strong. This will show that I am ready to be a woman.

When it is time for me to leave my *kapyk* after one moon cycle there will be much dancing and eating. First, my father will peel a cassava for me and I will make soft balls to bake in the sun. I must prepare my own fire and toast the cassava grains by myself and then take the grains to every family in the village. I will also make cassava drink for my family. Then I may wear the woman's feather necklace. My mother will give me my waistband. I will paint my face with *urucu*, pink paint, on my forehead and chin for the ceremony. I will then be a woman. The men will kill and cook a goat and the women will sing and dance until the sun rises again. Then I'll go home with my new husband. My name will then be Amatapu.

Kristin's Prom

Well, my prom was pretty cool. I went with this guy I know, Jared, who I'd been crushing on seriously for, like, the whole year. I spent a lot of time trying to decide whether to ask him or not. I was so petrified to make a fool out of myself, but finally my best friend, Katie, convinced me just to ask. If I'd known he'd say yes it would have saved me a lot of worry.

With that out of the way I could get down to the really serious planning. I'd been getting *Prom Magazine* all year, so I knew how much had to be done. I only had three months and most of my girlfriends had already got their dresses and stuff. First thing I did was book my hair and make-up. I was lucky – they get really booked up and you end up with a late appointment and no time to dress after, but I got the same time as Katie, so she planned to come back to my place after so we'd get ready together. We checked with our dates and they agreed to share a limo. Mom said she'd go shopping with me for my dress but that would have been a nightmare. Her taste and my taste are, like, totally out of sync. But my mom was a sweetie – she argued with my dad when he had a meltdown about how much it was all costing. She said that prom night for a girl is one of the best days of her life and that he shouldn't cheat me on it. That scored me the extra jewellery. In the end they let me go shopping with Katie and we both found awesome dresses. We went to Summerset Mall, three hours' drive away, so that no one else would have the same as ours. Mine was a Jovani, black with diamante straps and cut up the leg and it was, like, the best. I found diamante shoes with just a half-inch heel so I could still dance, and a bag to match. Dad gave me some diamante earrings, and Mom treated me to a facial, eyelash tint, manicure and wax.

Jared is not the type to dance or get dressed up, so when he agreed to go to the prom with me, I was psyched. I was going to get to see him in a tux! When we discussed plans, he told me that we could start at my house so our families could meet, and then we'd do pictures. Everything was perfect: my hair was all pinned up with corn rows in the back and these little ringlets around my face; I had pink lipstick, pink nails, and then he was going to bring a pink corsage. Katie and I were really psyched waiting for the limo.

When the guys arrived we took masses of photos and Jared was really polite and that to my mom; he even brought her some flowers. Then we all went to the Westerbrook Lodge for a really fancy meal, entrées and everything, but I didn't want to eat too much or I'd burst out of my dress!

We got to the prom at seven and you should have seen all the balloons, ribbons, banners and stuff. It was cold while we were queuing outside to go in, so Jared let me wear his tux jacket. I got so many compliments on my hair and dress. Even Jared's friends were saying nice stuff to me. I was soooo happy! Dancing was so romantic! We danced to almost every song, even the slow ones. When they announced prom King and Queen, guess who got it . . . We did! And during our dance together in front of everyone, he whispered, 'I wouldn't want to be anyone's king but yours!' Can you believe that? He said that in front of all of his jock friends and everything. It really made my heart melt. And when he dropped me back home he kissed me! We were in the newspaper the next day and I will never forget that night as long as I live.

Caitlin's special day

I'd been on at my parents for ages to get my ears pierced and they kept saying I had to wait until I was older. Then finally I got to! I'd not long turned thirteen, a teenager, and then I started my periods and my mum took me out, just me and her, to have my ears pierced. Afterwards we met up with the whole family to go out for dinner, which we don't do, hardly ever. And I got to choose which restaurant. They all made me feel really good, which was odd because having my period wasn't something I really liked, but they made me feel like it was something special. Mum and Dad gave me some gold earrings and they said nice things about me. I've not had an easy time with my periods, but I've got really good memories of that first time. At first I wasn't going to tell anyone, but then I did – I told my best friend about it, and now she wants her family to do something like that too.

Onawah's Sunrise Dance

My name is Onawah, which means 'wide awake one'. I am of the White Mountain Apache Tribe in Arizona. My people have lived here for many years, although things have changed a great deal in that time. I am thirteen years old and I am a woman now.

Plans for my *na'ii'ees*, my Sunrise Dance, started the month that we knew it was my time. At dawn we visited Udit, our medicine man, and I laid the eagle feather at his feet and he picked it up. Then we went to Elina's house and she too picked up the feather. This meant that she accepted to be my godmother. Udit and Elina worked with me for many hours, teaching me our sacred ways with stories and songs, showing me herbs and other ways of healing. Everybody helped, the men built a lodge, and for many weeks we prepared food and my mother worked on my buckskin dress. For six months I had to run, longer every day to build up my strength.

The Sunrise Dance lasts four days and nights and everyone is invited. There are too many sacred ceremonies, dances, songs, enactments and blessings to tell you about them all. Udit led it all and Elina stayed with me the whole time. First, she painted me all over with cornmeal and clay, which could not be washed off, and then she ran with me towards the east until I could go no further. Each day at dawn we ran to the east, each day a little further, and then back again. Udit called on our Great Spirit and the spirits of our ancestors to guide me and keep me safe. In dances, chants and stories I played the part of White Painted Woman, the first woman, so that I may know the ways of our women. With White Painted Woman's spirit inside me I learnt my healing powers and people came to me for blessings and healing. They also brought me gifts and their blessings. Every day we danced and sang for many hours, each day longer than before. Elina and my cousin, Kushala, danced with me, helping my spirit. Elina brought me food and drink. Each day I also ran as far as I could to the south and to the north and to the west, towards each of the four stages of life. My family made food and gifts for all our visitors. Every night Elina massaged me to 'mould' me into the shape of White Painted Woman so that I may become her. Udit led the dancing, drumming, chanting and praying, which went on through the night. Even as I became more tired than in death itself, I showed only my good spirits, for how I carried myself at Sunrise decided how I would be in adult life. Elina helped me to push away my giving-up thoughts and my bad thoughts towards others when all I wanted to do was be allowed to sleep. On the last day, when I had truly found my healing powers, I blessed everyone in my tribe with pollen, and everyone could gain good health by my touch. We ended with a feast.

I feel proud to be Apache – an Apache woman. I never realised before how much that would mean but now I do and Elina will be my special guide all my life. For all my relations, Ho!

Yasmin's celebration

My mother is Iranian and she often does things differently because of how she was brought up in her country. When my periods started, all the women got together and made me this sweet kind of eggy pancake, and we all talked and I got over being shy and asked all the questions that were going around my head, and it was lovely. I got presents too. I felt more grown-up after.

Katie's moment

My mum and me haven't been close in ages, but there was this one day that brought us back closer again. It was the day I started my monthlies. I was thirteen, and she just said, 'Welcome to my world,' with this really warm smile. Then she gave me a packet of pads and a heat pad, and we snuggled on the sofa with ice cream and a good film. It was nice.

Ilana's bat mitzvah

Hi, my name's Ilana and I've just turned twelve. I live in Golders Green in North London with my mum, dad, older brother and our dog Zipora (which means bird – go figure!). Anyway, last month I had my bat mitzvah, but there's not much to tell. I'm Jewish and I suppose you could call us practising Jews, although we're nothing like as religious as some round here. Anyway, according to Jewish Law every girl becomes bat mitzvah when she turns twelve, which means that we have to obey God's commandments, fast at Yom Kippur and stuff – before that we're just kids and of course you're supposed to obey God's laws, but it's more your parents' fault if you don't. Someone said that bat mitzvah means

'responsible female', so I guess that's what I am now. The boys, they don't
have their bar mitzvah until they are a year older and even that's too
early in my opinion. Have you ever met a responsible thirteen-year-old
boy? I know I haven't. Anyway, you should have seen the big deal they
made when my brother had his bar mitzvah. Months of classes learning
Hebrew and studying the Torah; that bit I wouldn't want, or having to
read from the Torah and lead the prayers in the synagogue. But the party
– you should have seen the fuss they made. Caterers, a band, two hundred
guests; you'd have thought he'd done something really special, not just get
a year older. And the presents – he could have made a small fortune on
eBay if he'd not wanted to pile them up and gloat. All I got was a charm
bracelet and a few candles and a little party at home with Mum and all
my 'aunties'. I suppose some of the things they said were kind of nice, like
my Aunt Rachel saying I was a credit to the family. Still, I wanted it to be
more special like my brother's, not just to make it fair but to make it feel
like I'm as important.

Meena's celebration

Hi, my name is Meena. My mum is English and my dad is Indian and we
live in England. I was born here. My dad moved over to England with his
parents and sisters when he was young, so I have loads of Indian family
– Awa, Tata, aunties, cousins. Because I've grown up here I feel English,
but I look Indian and sometimes I think it would be easier if I wasn't
half and half. I love my Indian side, though, especially when we all get
together, one big family. We have some great festivals too . . . Like the one
that happened when I started. That's definitely something English girls
miss out on. In India, when a girl has her first period there's a big fuss
with all the aunties – phone calls to everyone: 'Meena has come of age!'
It was the news of the day for a week or so. They all crowded over to our
place with food, and my dad was shooed out of the house. My mum was a
bit bemused I think, but she happily joined in with all the chat, advice and
feasting. My aunties told me about how it was in their village when they
were growing up, how a girl would be covered all over in coconut oil and
then given a special bath. After that she would have new clothes and there

would be a huge celebration like a wedding, kind of, and people would give her money and gifts. From then on, when it was her time of the month, she wouldn't be allowed in the kitchen or the temple. That was when it got heated, one auntie saying how she didn't hold with the whole business of treating women like they're unclean, and my other aunties saying how it was the tradition and would have been for a good reason. I was just crossing my fingers that my mum wouldn't say anything because I know she'd be dead set against it, but my Awa stopped it all by saying that it was nice not having to cook for a few days and being able to rest and have a bit of a break. That shut everyone up.

Anyway, my mother's brother is supposed to have some special responsibility for me now, but cos he's English and wouldn't know what it was all about my auntie offered her husband to stand in. I think it used to be that when a girl started it meant that she could marry or something, so her uncle was there to protect her from men until she did. I'm not sure about that bit. Anyhow, I'm not about to get married any time soon. All the attention was nice, though, and we had a real laugh. It started with them all giving me advice about my monthlies and being a woman and that, but it got sillier and sillier and then it got quite rude – even my auntie who's really proper. I'd never heard them talking like that. I liked being treated like one of them. It felt really special to be a woman – well, I'm not a woman yet, but I'm going to be.

I'm not sure what the girls at school would have made of it, though – having your period is something that is whispered about and everyone's embarrassed. Mind you, I would have thought my aunties were like that too and they're not, so maybe . . .

Charlotte's confirmation

My name is Charlotte Wilson, but soon it will be Charlotte Teresa Wilson. That'll be after my confirmation next Sunday when we take the name of our favourite saint. I like Teresa because she didn't find it easy to be a good Catholic and neither do I. My whole family is Catholic, and when I was a baby I was baptised. Now that I'm nearly twelve the promises that my parents and my godparents made for me at my baptism, well, I can make them for myself. We have to learn all about our faith in special classes, catechism classes, every week after church. We're supposed to prepare for everything to do with being an adult in the Catholic Church. Sometimes the classes can be a bit boring, but we still manage to have fun. We each have a sponsor who is a grown-up who helps during all the time that we are preparing for our confirmation. I've got my Aunt Lucy – she's my mother's little sister and she's much younger than my mum. We get along really well and she understands what it's like growing up – you know, growing up and being Catholic – much better than my own mum. Lots of my friends aren't Catholic and they can be a bit mean sometimes when I can't do the same things as them on Sundays because of my religion and everything. My best friend, Susie, she doesn't make a big deal out of it, though; once she even said that she wished she could have a special ceremony like we do.

I'm really looking forward to my confirmation day – well, mostly I am. I've got a really pretty, new, white dress and Mum will put flowers in my hair. We'll all be doing it together, my catechism class. I'm a bit nervous because the bishop asks us questions to see if we're ready and I'm sure I'll forget stuff. My sponsor will be there too, though, so that will help. There'll be a special church service and everyone will come, and the bishop will put this special oil on my forehead and then with his hand on top of my head he will pray and ask the Holy Spirit to enter me. I wonder if I'll feel different then ... Next the bishop gives us all our Holy Communion – that's a sip of wine and a wafer of bread, which is what Jesus did to his disciples at the last supper, and we're supposed to think of it like receiving the body and blood of Jesus Christ. I think the wine is watered down, though. There'll be a big party afterwards, and I've asked Mum to make my favourite lemon cheesecake, and it'll be my special day all that day. Once I've been confirmed, as well as my birthday I have my saint's day, which for me is October fifteenth, which is a bit like another birthday. My sister was confirmed last year and Mum and Dad gave her a beautiful silver necklace – it was a locket with a cross on it that opened and she could put a picture inside. She's got a photo of her boyfriend inside, but only I'm supposed to know that. I hope they give me a locket too.

Kali's coming of age

Hi, my name is Kali and I just did this amazing thing. My mum asked me if I would like a 'Coming of Age' ceremony, and at first I was, like, no way, but then after we talked about it I thought it might be kinda cool. I don't think I'll tell my friends at school about it, though; my best friends I would but not the others – I don't think they'd get it. My mum has always been into weird stuff like chanting and solstices and stuff. We can hardly sneeze without her lighting a candle for it! Anyway, that's just my mum, and I've kinda grown used to it.

So, my ceremony. Well, my body's been changing in the last while, and my moods too. God, sometimes I just feel so peed off, and they just treat me like a child, and, well, I just can't help myself – I can get really mean. Then some mornings I cry for absolutely no reason. I think more about how I look, get embarrassed more easily. I know it's all normal but it's a lot to deal with on top of school, and judo, and my irritating brother. Anyway, I'm changing, and Mum said she'd like to do something with me to make that feel special. I wasn't sure what she meant, but I really got into it once we got started.

We picked a date for my ceremony – May Day, just before my thirteenth birthday. Then we invited my godmother and my favourite aunt to come over and help me decide what to do. We started out really serious, but then it got all giggly as they talked about some of the things they did when they were my age. We had masses of ideas, but my godmother kept saying, 'Keep it simple. Keep it simple.' Mostly it was my mum who designed the ceremony, and my godmother offered to lead it. There was quite a lot to prepare, so we met up again a few times before the day. I got to know my aunt and my godmother in a different way – it was nice.

I made invitations for my family, my best friend, my judo teacher, my sort-of-boyfriend, one of my cousins; I wasn't sure about inviting my grandparents 'cos I knew this wasn't their thing, but I did in the end and I'm glad 'cos my granny even cried when she was asked.

I was really nervous on the day, but mostly I was busy with getting everything ready. My godmother stayed over the night before, and she and Mum helped me dress and do my hair, which I'm not sure if it made me feel a bit babyish. I began to feel really special too, especially when I could hear people starting to arrive downstairs.

When it was time, my godmother tied a ribbon around my mum's hand and then around my hand and led us down the stairs and out into the garden, and everyone followed. They stood in a circle, and we stood in the middle and we lit a candle – well, how could we not with my mum and all?! Then I read this piece I had written about my life so far, and then my godmother gave me some scissors and I cut the ribbon that was tying me and my mum together. Next I was supposed to say something to my mum about cutting myself free but still wanting her nearby, but I totally couldn't at first 'cos of feeling all choked up. Then she said something to me, which I can't even remember now, it was all so intense. Then she joined the circle and I stayed in the middle while everyone took a turn to say something to me, their wishes and blessings for my journey from being a girl to a woman. I thought I'd find it really embarrassing, but the things people said, it was like they really knew me and wanted all these good things for me. It just felt, I dunno, really lovely. Then we put on this wicked piece of music, one I really like to dance to, and everyone danced in the circle. It was like a party, and a huge relief, and we blew out the candle and went inside for this feast of all my favourite foods that me, Mum and my aunt had made.

Things were different after that. Not in a big way, but inside I felt different. I feel like I'm behaving better. Mum and I aren't fighting as much, either. It's made it feel special – growing up.

A RITE OF PASSAGE FOR YOUR DAUGHTER

Everyone makes the journey of growing up, and each one of us needs acknowledgement and validation for our individual passage through the life stages. Rituals provide this; they act as milestones. Without ritual validation of our progress, we may lose our way or seek other less healthy ways of proving our maturation. Moving from the child stage to the adult stage in life means great changes in the psyche, and a rite of passage is one way to help facilitate this.

A significant shift is required to move from the psychology of a girl to that of a woman. If older women assist in this shift, and create an event to mark it, it is more likely that a girl will become a grown woman of vision rather than growing up into a woman-child. It is stressful to live an adult life and have the psychology of a child – although many do. It is far better for both the individual and the community to invest energy in the process of maturation of our adolescents, giving our girls a sense of what it is to be a woman, and guidance along their way towards becoming one.

We can celebrate our girls and guide them through adolescence by creating meaningful rites of passage that feel right for them now, in our culture, in our time. I long for this to become the norm again: for girls to look forward to a special celebration, surrounded by their community of family and friends, in acknowledgement of the fact that they are no longer children and are making their way towards adulthood.

The power of a rite of passage is derived from a number of elements: developing relationships with older women and being counselled by them, succeeding in a challenge, being witnessed, and some ritual way of marking the event. You may wish to team up with other mothers and their daughters for some steps of this journey.

Organising a rite of passage for a teenage girl means getting closely involved in her maturation process and investing time in preparing her for adulthood. She is to be taught, challenged and tested to prove herself ready to take a symbolic step towards young adulthood. This step is witnessed and celebrated in the eyes of her community. Girls report a positive shift in their sense of themselves when their maturation is acknowledged in this way.

Marriage usually follows a period of engagement, and much preparation goes into the wedding day; so, too, a puberty rite is a process, not a single event. It may take a year or more to prepare. So start thinking about it now. Begin to engage in some of the preparation activities outlined in the following pages so that your daughter starts to become comfortable with the idea of a rite-of-passage celebration.

. . . .

Preparing for a rite of passage shows a girl what is expected of her in growing up and publicly acknowledges her maturity.

. . . .

Sally's story

When Sally started her periods, her mother Clare wanted to do something to celebrate. Sally did not. She felt very private about it and didn't want anyone to know. Although her mother understood, she also wished she could find a way to do something special for her daughter.

Sally had been through a lot in recent years. She'd not been happy since starting secondary school, and some of the other girls picked on her. Normally a bouncy, bubbly girl, she lost confidence. Finally, one day she refused ever to go back to that school, and nothing would budge her. After much shouting and tears it was agreed that she could stay home until they could find her a new school. As she settled into learning from home, her confidence slowly began to return. She sat in her room playing on her computer a lot and designing clothes, and that made her feel better too. Now that she was no longer at school, some of her friends left her out of things socially, which was hurtful, but she made some new friends.

None of this had been easy for Sally's parents, who worried about how to help her make the best choices for her future. Sally had shown great courage: she refused to change herself so that she would fit in at school, and she refused to stay somewhere that was making her so unhappy. Instead, she looked for a way to change her situation so that she could be happy again. None of this was easy, though.

So when Sally's periods started, a clear sign of her growing up, her mother wanted to acknowledge how well she was doing with finding her own unique way in the world. When she offered Sally a family celebration in her honour, Sally was horrified by the suggestion. Clare thought she would have to give up the idea. However, she kept returning to the pages on the Rites for Girls website about how to organise a coming-of-age ceremony, and it felt so right; somehow she could not let go of the notion, and eventually she contacted me to arrange a telephone consultation.

Clare and Sally talked some more, and with me in the background supporting Clare by phone, mother and daughter co-created the most beautiful celebration. The full story of their preparations and final ceremony unfolds through this chapter.

Knowing where to start

Suppose you recognise the value of acknowledging that your daughter is growing up. How do you then go about introducing the idea to her? It's not normal, it's potentially embarrassing, and it's your idea – all of which are likely to have her running for her room.

Start by discussing a celebration she knows and enjoys. Ask your daughter what makes birthdays special for her, or another festival that you celebrate. Listen to her describe the traditions, all the little ways that have evolved in your family that make this a special day set apart from the rest. As well as the annual celebrations, talk about once-in-a-lifetime ceremonies like christenings, marriages and funerals. Point out how all cultures and all religions have ways of marking and celebrating these significant life events, and wonder together about why this might be important.

Tell her that in many cultures great significance is given to supporting the journey that children make towards adulthood. More attention is given to this transition than any other in many cases – a puberty rite is seen as more important than weddings or funerals. Tell her that you would like to celebrate her coming of age with her. Then pause. See what she says. Don't push it. Leave her to think about it.

If possible, don't wait until she is entering puberty to have this conversation. Growing up with an understanding and an expectation of something is much easier than having it suddenly land in your lap. Many girls shy away when first offered a rite of passage. It's not familiar, and teens can be wary of doing something that could be seen to be different or weird. When left to ponder the idea though, many girls embrace the prospect of being supported and celebrated, as long as they feel that they will be consulted over how it happens. Those mothers who gently persevere in working with their daughters towards finding some way of marking their coming of age are inevitably thanked by them for doing so later on.

Sally's story

As Sally entered her teens, she spent much more time with her friends. She began to avoid spending time with her family – it was a bit of a battle to get her to see grandparents or to come along to family events. Her friends were super-important to her. Sally's family recognised this but felt that sometimes the influence of her friends wasn't always healthy. They weren't a bad bunch, but they were all young too, and experimenting, and none of them cared for Sally's wellbeing quite like her own family did.

Clare, her mother, was worried that Sally was losing touch with the people who cared about her most, especially as it was at a time in Sally's life when she might need their guidance or loving presence. She knew she couldn't make Sally choose to spend time with them, but instinctively she felt that maintaining a connection was important. She wondered if a coming-of-age ceremony for her daughter might be a way . . .

*Clare talked to Sally again to find out why she was so set against the idea. It turned out that when Sally was first offered a celebration, she assumed that her friends would need to be there, and this was what caused her to reject the idea outright. The thought of certain family members being present also repelled her. So Clare talked to Sally about **why** she wanted to do something – that it was **for** Sally. She explained that how they did it and who was there could be up to Sally. Sally began to think about it differently. The idea began to hold some appeal once she felt that she could make sure that nothing embarrassing would happen and that the guests would only be the people that she felt comfortable with.*

Explaining the point of a rite of passage – what's in it for her?

A rite of passage is a way of saying, 'We see you, we support you, we acknowledge that you are growing up and can begin to shoulder responsibility for your own life, and we expect you to do so.'

A rite of passage creates a shift in how you see yourself. It also creates a shift in how you are perceived within your community of family and friends, and it can help a teen's parents to hand over to their daughter the responsibility for increasingly managing her own life – helping the whole family's dynamic to mature.

• •

A rite of passage gives a growing girl a sense of making the journey towards adulthood surrounded by people who care for her.

• •

A rite of passage is not just the ceremony

The following are the key elements that will help you in the planning process of your daughter's rite of passage:

A circle of women to participate and be witness to the girl's journey

Think about the significant women in your daughter's life – grandmother, aunt, godmother, older sister, older cousin, neighbour, friend's mother, teacher, coach, youth worker, tutor ...

Elders

Involving key women in your daughter's life who know and care about her validates her growing sense of self. Women allies, sharing stories, their wisdom and, above all, their time.

Is there a favourite granny or godparent? Actually, any willing wise woman will do! Go out of your way to foster this relationship. If there is an absence of women to call upon, then this initial stage may take a year or so while you seek out and invite one or two key women to involve themselves in your daughter's life.

Family history

Who are your people, and where do you come from? Knowing about our ancestors, the common threads that we share with the women who lived before us, adds to our sense of who we are.

How much does your daughter know of your life? And your mother's? And other women who have lived before her? Find photos to show her. Take care not to use the stories as moral tales or as evidence of how easy she has it (she doesn't feel that way). Share the high times and the low times and let her know about some of the teenage struggles you had. Is there anything she ought to know that might help her to make sense of how things are in your family? Give her roots. Tell her what you know of the women who have come before her – gifting her the aural tradition of passing family stories down the generations.

Segregation

Time with other girls at a similar stage, together with an older woman to guide them in considering the changes and challenges that adulthood brings.

Girls Journeying Together provides this, but you can organise it in other ways. Gather a group of your daughter's friends and do something they enjoy, using it as a vehicle for allowing discussions to happen. Perhaps an afternoon of nail-painting and chat, a country bonfire, or after watching a DVD together.

Seclusion

Time alone for reflection. No books, mobile phones or similar distractions.

Many young people have very little time alone for contemplation, which is substantially different from when they isolate themselves because they are miserable. So rarely are children parted from their peers or their technology that they can be quite fearful of the prospect of time spent quietly alone. You may need to start small – half an hour alone in the garden pondering her favourite childhood memories, or an hour in the bath to think about which women she admires. Once your daughter learns that she is able to spend time alone, she will discover how this puts her in touch with herself. You have given her a life-gift if she makes friends with solitude.

Defining self-purpose

Your daughter taking some time to consider what kind of woman she wishes to become helps to orientate her towards her purpose.

This is about clarifying what is important to her in life, not just career choice – although this may be a part of it for some. What does she aspire to? Who does she admire? What kind of woman does she want to become? Who could become a mentor? If someone other than a parent asks her these questions, she will find different answers. It will involve dreaming and imagining her future; it may also entail writing or speaking a vow for herself. Often it is worth giving her time to mull this over, and then she can revisit it throughout life.

Challenge

Some event or task that challenges her, takes her to some sort of edge so that when she succeeds, she can rightfully feel that she has tested herself and proved that she has moved forward on her journey towards womanhood.

This gives the rite meaning. The challenge needs to be chosen with your daughter in mind – what matters to her? What would feel like an achievement for her? With boys this traditionally involves a physical feat, and this may be true for some girls too. Alternatively, her challenge could be to travel somewhere alone, take sole care of an elderly relative, perform in some way, walk to the coast, give a week of her life to supporting a new mother, organise an event, climb a mountain, write and record a song, or sail single-handed around the world!

An end, as well as a beginning

Some childish things are being left behind, and new adult responsibilities are being taken up.

With change comes grief, so expect to feel sad about your little girl growing up, and expect some ambivalence from your daughter too. Symbolic acts can help to give form to the conflicting feelings of loss and excitement – you may want to make a photo album together of her first decade, pass on old toys, or visit an old favourite childhood haunt. Once the loss is felt and honoured, the possibility of celebrating the new stage is opened up.

Planning the ceremony

This is as important as the event itself and will often throw into light the issues that need to be resolved in order to move forward. It serves the daughter to be given sole responsibility for some aspects of the preparation and to be encouraged to draw on the support of those around her if required. It serves the mother to hand over some of the responsibility to her daughter and to be supported in letting go by those around her.

There's nothing like a bit of joint decision-making to highlight the areas where you and your daughter have differences. This is important work for you both, and there are no prizes for just coping, so get help. Transitions are rarely smooth, and the glitches indicate the areas requiring growth. There is added meaning to the whole process when the two of you apply effort, ingenuity and changes in behaviour in order to find solutions to your differences.

The ceremony

Once all the above elements have been covered, which may take a year or more, then you can consider a suitable ritual or celebration to mark your daughter's coming of age. You may like to design the ceremony with your daughter, or she may prefer you to create it for her.

Sally's story

Clare read and reread the list for how to prepare for a rite of passage, stuck for ideas on how to carry it out when her daughter was still largely reluctant to engage with any of it. Here are her initial thoughts.

A circle of women and elders

Family life was so busy, and there was no obvious group of women who could offer their support to Sally. Then Clare thought of Jan, an old family friend of many years who Sally always seemed to enjoy seeing. Even though Jan lived in

France, with no children herself, and wasn't likely to have ever been part of a coming-of-age ceremony before, Clare phoned her to see if she would help. To Clare's surprise Jan was curious and willing, and they talked about her staying for a couple of days next time she was in the country.

Segregation

As Sally had been through a difficult time with her friends, Clare couldn't see how time spent with peers would appeal to Sally right now.

Seclusion and defining self-purpose

These were easier in Sally's case, as she had spent lots of time at home when in between schools, pondering what she wanted to do with her life.

Challenge

Sally herself came up with the idea of designing and making her own outfit. She wasn't sure if she would want to wear it on the night in front of others, though.

Preparation

Clare contacted me for support and we discussed her ideas and Sally's needs, and then Clare mulled things over with Sally. Sally didn't really want to be that involved in the preparation except to have the power of veto. She wanted to make sure that she would feel okay with whatever her mother was planning and that only people that she felt comfortable to have there would be invited. In the end, they both decided to take the risk of inviting Sally's maternal grandmother as an elder in their family.

Symbols

Clare had a necklace that her mother had given to her when she was a girl and she wanted to pass it on to Sally. After much vacillating, she also decided to give Sally a pet snake – much hankered for but until now denied to her. By entrusting Sally with the care of another creature, Clare wanted to show her that she now considered her to be ready to take on this responsibility.

The Ceremony

Several months later, Clare contacted me to discuss her ideas for the ceremony.

Preparing your daughter for the journey

Although your focus may be on the final ceremony, what goes on before it is of primary importance. The many ways that you prepare your daughter and strengthen your relationship with her using all the parenting tools suggested throughout this book are an essential precursor to your ceremonial celebration of her.

When do you start preparing? Now!

What do you do? Much of what you need to do has been covered in the chapters leading up to this one. Whatever the age of your daughter, spend time alone with her, have Mother–Daughter Dates, cultivate her special relationships with older women, keep family mealtimes, encourage her to do the things that engage her. Point out her strengths to her, invite her questions, talk about womanly things and teach her how to take care of herself. Have fun together.

Who can support her on her journey? All the women in her life. See if there is someone in particular you feel she can share her dreams and concerns with, and ensure that she can spend time with her. You may want to formally ask if she will take on the role of mentor to your daughter.

Prepare yourself. You cannot comfortably guide your daughter through terrain that you have not visited yourself. Your challenge is to seek *your* right answers to these questions for yourself first:

- How do you live a meaningful, fulfilling life according to your morals and values?
- How might you resolve unfinished business from your childhood?
- What more do you need to attend to in yourself to become a whole and happy grown-up woman?

As mentioned in Chapter Two, answering these questions may be done in quiet contemplation, with friends, in conversation with someone close, or with a counsellor. We all benefit from reflecting on our own lives, and it will strengthen your ability to support your daughter's maturation.

As she approaches puberty . . . Now is the time to focus on preparing your daughter for her first bleed and considering some way of marking this.

Talk to her about practical things. Periods, peer pressure, cultural influences, body image, managing stress, mood swings, sex, education, dreams and future plans, personal heritage, values, how to manage money, creative ways of self-expression, giving back, health, fitness, good eating, self-care. I hope this book gives you what you need to do this.

Share the fun stuff of being a woman. Whatever that may be for you – girly nights, eat out, stay in to watch a film together, invite friends to a clothes-swap evening, go to the cinema, pass on a favourite read, share cinnamon toast at midnight, have your hair done, go shopping somewhere unusual, feed the ducks, have a brew and a chat, splash out on a pampering session, buy luxury chocolates, hike in the woods, have a pyjama day.

Help her to feel positive about her changing body. Show her how to take care of her body with food, exercise, sleep, hygiene and relaxation. Run her a fragrant candlelit bath, hold off on negative comments about her physical appearance, have healthy appetising food in the house, don't create a culture of dieting, notice her clothes (even if they are not what you would have chosen), treat her to a make-up session, massage her shoulders, go for a walk in nature together.

Encourage her to express herself. Give her a lockable diary, sketchbook, voice recorder, lump of clay . . .

Stay deeply involved, and create happy moments together. Your teen needs you, no matter what she might say at times. Find a sensitive way to walk alongside her as she makes her unique journey towards womanhood. Give her space, but give her your attention too. Make moments to remember. Give her opportunities to prove to herself and other people that she is successfully making her passage to womanhood.

Discuss how she would like you to acknowledge her growing up. Talk about how your responsibility for her will ebb as her responsibility for herself grows. A rite-of-passage ceremony can help that process. Creating a coming-of-age ritual is a very powerful way of asking your daughter to step into greater maturity, and at the same time of symbolically helping you to let go. A rite of passage signifies a gateway, a significant step towards adulthood, providing an empowering and poignant marker along your daughter's path towards becoming a young woman.

* *

Never hesitate to celebrate – do not wait for the perfect moment. You can make the moment!

* *

Co-creating your daughter's ritual ceremony

A rite-of-passage ceremony or ritual can be as involved as our other rites around marriage, naming or funerals, or it can be delightfully simple. I treasure the ordinary, the everyday and the reassurance that familiarity brings. Something commonplace, done consciously, can be every bit as sacred as an out-of-the-ordinary ritual, and it might appeal to your teenager more. However, the presence of witnesses adds weight, so encourage her to think of who she might like to have with her.

A meaningful ritual could involve:

- A special meal with a pause for a few well-chosen words.
- A mother-and-daughter trip to some long-dreamed-of destination.
- A visit to an old childhood haunt, to remember and talk of hopes for the future.
- Grandma handing on a family treasure.

A ritual can be normal and special at the same time. It can be meaningful without having to include things that would make your daughter cringe. Teenagers are notoriously easy to embarrass. Sensitivity to this is essential in allowing her to be fully present at her own event. Equally, magic happens – in the right setting, people will suddenly feel moved to say or do things that they would never normally feel comfortable with. Trust that, if you keep it simple and sincere, it will be powerful and meaningful. Whether you design something for her yourself, or you and your daughter create something together, it's important to tailor her rite of passage to suit her. You are looking for a balance between it feeling comfortable to her and it having an element of challenge.

As we live in a culture that does not have any clearly defined ways of marking and celebrating the transition from girl to woman, we have the task and luxury of creating our own. When parents contact me for guidance on organising a puberty rite of passage for their child, I always begin by asking what they hope to gain from such an event. Their answers help us to design the ceremony and celebration:

'I want to make a fuss of her. It's a difficult stage of life and I want her to know that we're there for her.'

'I did lots of things when I was a teenager that I'd hate for my daughter to do. It was like I was trying to prove that I was grown-up. I don't want her to have to do that. I want her to have healthier ways of knowing that she's becoming an adult.'

'Make her grow up a bit. She's often telling us to stop treating her like a child, and I'd like to, but she has to stop behaving like one. I think something like a puberty rite will make her realise that she has to step up if she wants us to trust her. I think it might help us to see her differently too – treat her more as an adult.'

'I want her to see how many people care for her. That she's not alone. And it gives us a reason to talk about what growing up means, but also what is required of her, and to tell her what is great about her, boost her confidence. Good excuse for a party too!'

What follows is a list of the key elements to include in your ceremony, but first we start with you. Allow your intuition to guide you towards what would be right for your daughter. You may wish to mull it over with other female relatives and close women friends too. Trust that your knowledge of your daughter will guide you in how to honour her emerging womanhood.

Your ceremonial celebration checklist:

- Begin by thinking about what gives her pleasure – go to her comfort zone first.
- What is important to her – what would give this rite meaning?
- What does she need at this stage in her life?
- Consider what might take her to an edge, just out of her comfort zone – this adds transformative power to the ritual.
- Think about who could be supportive to her in this.
- Who are the important females in her life? Who else could be involved or invited?
- How can the important males in her life play their part? How would you like to include them?
- Who will lead the ritual? You, a friend, a family member or a celebrant?

- What could you do that would make her feel special?
- Would some element of surprise serve to heighten the experience? An unexpected guest, an extra challenge, some words from a grandmother, something hand-made for her . . . ?
- What is the most suitable venue? Where would be comfortable, private, special?
- Dress: a sense of occasion can be created by dressing in a celebratory manner.
- Photographs: although it can be lovely to have a visual record, the taking of photographs can intrude and interfere with the experience of being really present, so decide beforehand what you want and communicate this clearly to everyone. You could perhaps designate one person to discreetly snap away, with copies made available to others afterwards.

If you are co-creating this event with your daughter, then **do not rush or impede her** in the planning. For some mothers this is hard. Once you have it all arranged, make space for the unexpected. Things often don't go according to plan, so it is useful if you and your daughter are clear about what is most important to you, hold on to that, and then be willing to make it up as you go along if other things don't run quite as intended.

Key ingredients for her ceremony

You are creating something unique for your daughter, mixing the constituents to suit her taste. So, although I outline the key ingredients, the final recipe is yours.

All rituals need a beginning, a happening and an end, followed by feasting. This can be as simple as lighting a candle, speaking, blowing the candle out and sharing a hot chocolate. It can also involve a lot more.

The welcome – put guests at their ease by welcoming them, perhaps remembering those who cannot be there, saying what you are gathered for (to mark your daughter's stepping away from childhood and towards adulthood) and explaining what is going to happen. People will also appreciate being told what is going to be expected of them. You may want to say something about how you and your daughter have prepared for this event.

Physical contact – this can help to bring intimacy to the gathering. Although often spontaneous, it can also set the tone as long as it feels comfortable for your daughter: holding hands, washing your daughter's feet, massaging her hands, a hug, a kiss or placing hands on her heart are all powerful.

The happening – this is where you do something that gives meaning and purpose to the event. The possibilities are infinite. Your daughter may have prepared something for this part of the ceremony, or she may have an intention for herself that she would like to speak aloud. You may have given her a challenge to perform. Others close to your daughter may have been asked to participate in some way.

Offerings, blessings and well-wishing – words spoken in a ritual setting carry great weight. This can be a good time to offer words of support, words of acknowledgement of a girl's skills and strengths, words of warning and words of wisdom.

The symbolic gift – give your daughter a gift to signify and acknowledge her achievement, to serve as a talisman and to remind her of the power of what she has undergone. Anything that is used or exchanged within the ritual context becomes imbued with special meaning, so the time and thought that you give to the choice of gift is more important than its cost. Gift ideas: a hand-made purse filled with treasures; a piece of family jewellery; a heart-shaped stone; a letter written from the heart; some significant trinket from your past; a poem; a tree planted somewhere special; a moonstone; strands of her hair, your hair and her grandmother's hair woven into a plaited thread; a family heirloom; a voucher to have her ears pierced; something home-made; a box.

Signifiers – you may also want to include in the ceremony representations of things that have significance for this time in her life:

objects to represent growth, nourishment, water of life, air we breathe, fire of change, passage of time, ancestors . . .

Closing – it is important to let people know when the ceremony has ended. Thank them for being there. Blow out a candle, blow your daughter a kiss, clap, hug, sing her name, shout three cheers – whatever seems right.

Merrymaking – finish with a celebration, feasting on favourite foods, with special people, music, and merrymaking. Dancing – some would say there must be dancing! Or music at least, and singing.

Sally's ceremony and celebration

The smell of flowers filled the living room, a huge cake sat on the table in the corner, the double doors were open onto the garden where a small group of women sat around a low table. Clare lit the candle on the table, beside which were a few photos of Sally as a baby, as a little girl, and now. On either side of Clare were her two daughters, Sally and Lily. Next to Sally was Jan, the family friend who had travelled over especially, and beside her was Sally's maternal grandmother and one other long-standing family friend. Clare thanked everyone for coming and explained that there would be a chance for everyone to say something, and then a belly dancing teacher would perform and teach everyone a little dance, with cake to finish.

Clare began by reading to Sally a long letter that she had spent many weeks writing and had made into a beautiful book tied with a ribbon. This set the tone and inspired additional heartfelt messages for Sally from the other women. Her sister had drawn an amazing multicoloured picture. Jan talked about watching Sally growing up, about what she had observed, and she listed the qualities she saw in her. Sally's struggles were acknowledged, and so were her strengths. Most astonishing was when Sally's grandmother stood up to read a poem she had written about Sally – the grandmother she so nearly didn't invite as this was so far from anything she thought her grandmother would ever do. The poem was funny and intimate and moved everyone to tears.

Sally hadn't felt sure about wearing the clothes she had designed and made, so she had taken pictures to show everyone instead. Everyone's response was so genuinely enthusiastic on seeing the photos, that Sally was persuaded to put her new outfit on. It was a sweet ending to the ceremony. Just before the candle was blown out, Clare presented Sally with her snake, which created a frisson of nervous fascination all round.

The Arabian dance teacher arrived, beautifully dressed in scarves and shimmering sequins, and performed a mesmerising dance. Much mirth and merriment accompanied her session of teaching everyone some of the moves plus a short dance. By this time, everyone was very ready for the cake, which Sally's sister had baked for her. The evening ended with everyone sitting around on cushions on the floor of the sitting room, eating, drinking and laughing.

When I spoke to Sally a few years later, she recalled the ceremony with fondness and said she was pleased her mother had made it happen, despite her resistance at the time. She often thought about the lovely things people had said, especially when she felt uncertain about herself. She was surprised at how she had felt different afterwards, like she was entering a new chapter in her life; and her mum had treated her differently too.

A puberty rite of passage shows your daughter that you recognise she is growing up, which in turn helps her to step into a new more mature phase of her life. The way in which you acknowledge her must be tailored to who she is and can be as simple as a celebratory meal out, a special mother–daughter day or a more elaborate event with special guests, words, food and a gift.

Invitation

I am currently gathering stories of coming-of-age ceremonies and puberty rites of passage to support mothers and their daughters to celebrate at this vital time in a girl's life. If you or your daughter feel moved to share your own experience, however simple, quirky or elaborate, please send your story to me at info@ritesforgirls.com describing your preparations, how you celebrated and what it meant to you both. I would really appreciate your help in inspiring others.

Parting thoughts

TEENAGERS ARE GREAT!

I often hear comments about how infants bring a sense of wonder back into our lives. With teenagers, however, the focus tends to be on how they irritate us and less on how their behaviour can remind us of what is truly important in life. For example:

- Taking myself and my feelings really, really seriously.
- Fighting for my right to live how I want.
- Caring a great deal about my friends.
- Questioning authority.
- Seeking excitement.
- Experimenting with how I look.
- Wondering who I am.
- Taking risks.
- Sleeping until I no longer feel tired.
- Eating what I really fancy.
- Courting new friendships.
- Testing limits.
- Acting on impulse.
- Learning by doing.
- Going for what I want.
- Winging it.
- Giggling.

- Trying new things.
- Railing at life's injustices.
- Believing that a better world is within our grasp.

RAISING YOUR TEEN WELL

Adolescence is an exhilarating, sensitive and precious time. It takes effort to stay in close connection with your daughter as you let her go. The teenage years call for her increasing independence but this requires a bigger role for parents, not a diminishing one. Your daughter wants you alongside during this vulnerable phase; she needs you more than ever, despite how it may sometimes seem. We see how the particular challenges of adolescence cause our teenage girls to be increasingly susceptible to mental health problems. You cannot protect your daughter from the world but you can prepare her to take her place as a strong, sure and capable young woman.

Parenting an adolescent is exciting, but is also demanding and can require every ounce of your patience, resilience and love. It also takes your time. Committing to a regular Mother–Daughter Date lets her know how important she is. It also serves to keep you connected and able to offer her the support that she needs. Every mother can transmit and inspire from her female knowledge and wisdom in her own unique way. For your daughter to accept your guidance you need to be in a committed and trustful relationship with her, which can require you to grow up yourself.

Bringing up healthy girls is not to be done alone. Draw on the insights of others. Your own parents may have some wisdom gained from hindsight. Your friends who have children older than yours will also have experience that could help. The mothers of your daughter's friends will undoubtedly be sharing some of the questions and concerns that you have. Teachers, youth workers and anyone else who works with young people will have knowledge that may be of use to you. If you run into really challenging problems, don't hesitate to call on the support of counsellors or therapists specifically trained to work with teens; they can help to prevent things from getting a lot worse. Search your intuition and your experience as you too have been through this stage. When you tap into what you have learned and combine it with what you know of your daughter, and your love for her, you will find answers. It's an art: knowing what to say or do, when to act and when to leave alone. Give your child the benefit of your full attention when it's needed and give yourself the support of those around you. Encourage her to find mentors so that she has plenty of opportunity for guidance and support from adults other than her own parents. As coming-of-age groups become commonplace, every girl will grow up expecting this extra support as she grows through her adolescence.

Every birthday I am struck by how swiftly my children grow. I still feel like a new mum, so how is it that I have a teenager who has grown into a young man, and no longer lives with us, and two others who will soon follow? I do want to give my children the wings to fly, but their lives seem to be flying by. In the tough early days of colic, sleep deprivation and constantly keeping a careful eye, I used to whisper to myself, 'One day, eighteen. One day, eighteen.' That eighteenth birthday is long gone for my eldest. The teen years are tough also, in their own way, but fortunately I know that they too will pass all too quickly. Older mothers tell me how precious those child-rearing years now seem, occupying such a brief period of their lives. Childhood is so short and I don't want to blink and miss it. I want the wisdom to stop and look properly at what my child is showing me (even though the meal needs cooking), to gather my daughter in my arms until the tears stop flowing (even though the phone is ringing), to listen closely to the intricate details of the latest new idea (even when I am distracted with thoughts of my own), and to read another chapter of the bedtime story (even though I want to spend time with her dad).

I hear from parents whose children have run into difficulties, wishing that they'd noticed sooner and given better attention earlier. None of us are immune from life's challenges and just because we might have difficulties in parenting a teen, does not mean we are poor parents. When the difficulties do arise, however, it helps enormously if your relationship with your child is alive and strong.

I hope this book will take away the dread that some parents have as their child heads for the teen years. Parenting a teenager can be immensely rewarding. Teens are vital, adventurous, questioning and self-conscious. Being closely involved in a teen's life can prompt us (or force us!) to re-evaluate our own priorities, question our assumptions and remember the reasons for our choices. Being witness to a young person forming her 'self' is a great privilege. Remember that it's not in your job description to be your teen's best friend or for her to like you all the time. You are here to love her, guide her and gradually let her go. You are joining a (r)evolutionary network of women working to restore natural female beauty, power and sexual dignity to girls and women for the benefit of boys and girls, men and women, for generations to come. You can make a difference, a big difference, by harnessing your own deep beauty, power and wisdom and passing it on to your daughter.

Hold your child in an open hand.

Rites for Girls

Acknowledgements

First, I want to thank my mother, Rosanne, for giving birth to me in so many ways; my grandmothers, Ione and Doris; their mothers, Gilian and Mary; and all the mothers in the great long line of ancestors that have come before me. Next is Cara, my own daughter, who is teaching me about womanhood and carries forward the rare maternal gene from our original Yemeni mother. No pressure, Cara!

Two boys came before Cara, Marcus and Callum, who taught me about infinite love and who have generously tidied and vacated our home for every Girls Journeying Together and always asked how it went. And our dear Theo whose death broke my heart but also channelled my energy towards creating Rites for Girls. This book is published one day after Theo's anniversary, ten years on. And I have my beloved, Jaimie, who stands beside me with his hand at my back.

Some other important men: my dad, who taught me how to follow my heart; Justin Vaughan (my first love); Andy Blamey (who I grew up with); Colin (who hit me repeatedly – but never again).

Thank you to the girls at school who bullied me, and the teachers who did nothing about it: I'd probably never be doing this work without you. Trish Maude, my gymnastics coach, a lifeline through childhood. Kum-Kum Bhavnani, who asked if I was okay when I wasn't. Tess Adkins, who took care of me as King's College senior tutor, enabler and our marriage celebrant.

Some great men and women inspire and support me, starting with May Brenner (living on), Linde Raisbeck (who first saw me), Susannah and Ya'Acov Darling-Khan, Gabrielle Roth (who invited me to teach) and Geoff Lamb (who won't stop asking me what I need). Melissa Michaels (who encouraged me so warmly) and, above all, Steve Biddulph, a mentor who cheers me on, grounds me, and lends his weight and wisdom to my work. Naomi kick-started Girls Journeying Together for her daughter Juno; and Helena, who is a joy to work beside in launching Rites for Girls Facilitator Training into the world. Ruby and Emily. Mairi and Georgie. In my work with preteens and adolescents, the girls have taught me about what they need in order to grow wholesomely into spirited young women. To each one of my Girls Journeying Together girls, thank you. I look forward to meeting your daughters.

For being my girlfriends: Jo Hamblin, Sarah Wentworth, Rachel Heap, Yamuna Thiru, Julia Bucknall, Erica Wagner and Zanna Brindle.

For being my women friends: Frances, Julia, Kay, Elizabeth, Fanny, Dawn, Janey, Nomes, Ness, Sara, Sally, Maria, Jen, Sarah, Tanya, Rebecca, Annie, Vania, Naphia, Mandy, Nichola, Emily, Donna, Caz, Tamara, Shell, Ayumi, Joy, Alia, Michelle, Linda-La, Clare, Annabel, Marien, Emma, Flora, Kate and many more.

For being my sisters from another mother: Mairi Stones, Jo Carder, Julia Ventham, Frances Mills.

For being my sister from the same mother: Heidi – oh! what we've shared.

My brother Russell, for always remembering our Theo, and my other brother, Julian, for being himself. Tess, Yurim, Caitlin and Juno. John and Anna and Olwen, whanau. My goddaughters Molly, Izzy and Hetty.

In writing this book: Brad, who opened the publisher's door; Andy, my lifelong pal-with-a-pen who gave me the title; Frances, who nourished me; Michelle and Alia, for gathering in our children. Des for his advice. My publishers Nikki Read and Amanda Keats at Robinson. My reading team: Zanna, Jo, Mairi, Emma, Jaimie, Anna, Andy, Jim and Cara. Helen for her tireless attention to detail and most especially Patricia Patterson-Vanegas, who midwifed me through the second stage: you understood what I was trying to do and helped me to shape the wood when all I could see were trees and stayed with me right to the final push.

Your book will sit on my shelf with the few books I keep to reread every now and then. Thank you, Kim, it is such a gift you are giving us moms – helping us love our teens. I love having children, but I've been dreading the teen years. I have such a different attitude now and feel that, although it won't be easy, I can enter these years a bit more confidently and, dare I say, joyfully.

Cara Bishop

I have never understood the pressures on my daughter until today. It gives me a lot of tools to be a better dad.

Jim

With warmth, compassion and humour, From Daughter to Woman *offers guidance and encouragement to women of all ages in one of the most important journeys of their lifetime.*

Andrew Graham

In From Daughter to Woman *Kim invites us as mothers to develop a different relationship with our daughters, one that takes us on a journey into our own womanhood as well as that of our beautiful daughters. It challenges modern notions of difficult teens and supports us to develop deep and lasting relationships based on respect for the emerging woman we have birthed into the world. This book is a teacher, guide, and companion through a period in our daughters lives which can be easy to dread. Kim shows us how to embrace, enjoy and most of all celebrate it.*

Mairi Stones

I wish this book had been available when I was growing up.

Anna Comino-James
Founder trustee Potential Trust

I love it when a wise voice gently reminds and teaches me about · that which is truly essential. From Daughter to Woman *is one of these voices. In a truly feminine style, Kim combines intellectual brilliance, intuitive wisdom, gentleness and love to produce a guide that not only explains how it is for our teenage girls, but empowers us to meet their needs as they grow up in a materialistic world that is full of confusing messages; a world that is increasingly overwhelming them with innumerable pressures and mounting stress. We, the adults, can help our girls to become the authentic, free and passionate women that our society needs.* From Daughter to Woman *is an indispensable tool in this most valuable process.*

Patricia Patterson-Vanegas
Founder and former editor of Juno Magazine